KU-218-848

Helen Stevenson grew up in South Yorkshire and studied modern languages at Somerville College, Oxford. She is a translator and the author of three novels, *Pierrot Lunaire*, *Windfall* and *Mad Elaine*. Since taking up full-time writing, she regularly reviews for the *Independent*. She now lives in London.

Acclaim for *Instructions for Visitors*:

'After a failed marriage, the author found herself in a village on the southwest tip of France. Its history was variegated – first the Romans, then the Spanish and finally the French all put their mark on the region. Before long, the village's beauty, langour and *laissez faire* pattern entrapped Stevenson ... Into this sensuous landscape steps Luc, and the picture alters. Luc is a painter, part-time dentist and local Lothario, whose former lovers see themselves as the old regime and insist on supervising the administrative details of the new. He is clever, bitter and angry, perfect for a woman drawn to men who are bad for her ... *Instructions for Visitors* segues between the diary, the confessional and the straightforward travel record ... this rich, slightly uneasy, mixture is what makes it so interesting. A beautifully tactile and reflective meditation on the outsider's experience of a community'
Elizabeth Buchan, *The Times*

'Like one of Luc's pictures, this memoir is striking for its bright images, its elegant originality, and its poignant understatements. Funny and perceptive, its reads sometimes like the guidebook it pretends to be, sometimes like a diary . . . Yet our heroine stays detached from her reader, hiding behind the artifice of her form as if she dare not quite confront her emotions any more than she can decide whether or not to stay in this very nearly irresistible place. For the source of her confusion, *cherchez l'homme*'
Sue Gaisford, *Harper's & Queen*

'Gradually, the descriptions of sensual awakenings in strange beds, of breakfasts in blistering heat on unshaded terraces, connect up with the interior terrain of autobiography. Helen Stevenson falls for Luc ... and struggles to make sense of the new life she has chosen ... this clever, gripping and elegantly written account of their life together ... [is] her elegy for the end of a powerful, life-shaping love affair'
Michèle Roberts, *Independent*

'Stevenson's village attains life beyond the stereotypes, a vividness that goes deeper than Gallic hauteur and great bread. Gradually we inhabit the bitter-sweet relationship with Luc, an ageless, arrogant and infuriating scion of the village and can see the place not only through her foreigner's eyes, but through his, a local whose horizons lower on the road out of the village . . . It is a grown-up affair, not the shallow, girlish solipsism of airport chick lit, but a complex series of misunderstandings, misinterpretations and tiny culture-tremors that eventually burst out into full-grown fissures. Stevenson makes it affecting because she tells it at an oblique angle, slipping in the poignancy between softly humorous evocations of village life'
Tom Lappin, *Scotland on Sunday*

'On the run from her marriage, Stevenson exchanges the comfortable existence of an expat in the south of France to shack up with an artist near the Spanish border. That her unpredictable lover also earns his living as the local dentist is one of the unexpected features of a tale that is not so much a memoir as an impressionistic portrait of bourgeois life in provincial France. The book begins as instructions for holidaying guests arriving at the author's house. But soon she is turning her novelist's eye on the town's characters – from the middle-class former revolutionary, content to reconcile his Marxism with sponging off his wife and sleeping around, to the malicious boutique owner who insists on dressing new girlfriends of her various ex-lovers. The result is as voyeuristically pleasurable as rooting through the owner's letters and photo albums in a rented cottage'
Sunday Times

'Helen Stevenson has written a brilliant memoir about how it feels to fall in love not only with a place, but also with the man who embodies it. Spending much of her time in the south-west of France where she owns a house, Stevenson finds herself falling in love with Luc – a painter, cowboy and dentist. While Luc has lived in *le village* all his life and is used to its slow, mysterious rhythms, Stevenson still has all the anxious get-up-and-go of a thirtysomething Englishwoman. In haunting, delicate prose, she explores the painful realisation that she will always be a stranger – to her lover and her home'
Eve

Also by Helen Stevenson

PIERROT LUNAIRE
WINDFALL
MAD ELAINE

INSTRUCTIONS FOR VISITORS

Helen Stevenson

BLACK SWAN

INSTRUCTIONS FOR VISITORS
A BLACK SWAN BOOK : 0 552 99928 8

Originally published in Great Britain by Doubleday,
a division of Transworld Publishers

PRINTING HISTORY
Doubleday edition published 2000
Black Swan edition published 2002

5 7 9 10 8 6 4

Copyright © Helen Stevenson 2000

The right of Helen Stevenson to be identified as the author
of this work has been asserted in accordance with sections 77
and 78 of the Copyright Designs and Patents Act 1988.

Condition of Sale
This book is sold subject to the condition that it shall not,
by way of trade or otherwise, be lent, re-sold, hired out or
otherwise circulates in any form of being or cover other
than that in which it is published and without a similar
condition including this condition being imposed on the
subsequent purchaser.

Set in 11/13pt Melior by
Falcon Oast Graphic Art Ltd.

Black Swan Books are published by Transworld Publishers,
61–63 Uxbridge Road, London W5 5SA,
a division of The Random House Group Ltd,
in Australia by Random House Australia (Pty) Ltd,
20 Alfred Street, Milsons Point, Sydney, NSW 2061, Australia,
in New Zealand by Random House New Zealand Ltd,
18 Poland Road, Glenfield, Auckland 10, New Zealand
and in South Africa by Random House (Pty) Ltd,
Endulini, 5a Jubilee Road, Parktown 2193, South Africa.

Printed and bound in Great Britain by
Clays Ltd, St Ives plc.

To all those whose stories enriched this account and whose lives touched mine, I am indebted with gratitude and great affection.

1. Instructions

Directions

Leave the motorway at the last exit in France, where the eastern blade of the Pyrenees shelves down to the sea. The peaks to the west are granite hard; but from mountain to hill to lower slope the rock softens, first to scree and stones, then later into crumbly earth. Down on the beach the endless tiny lapping movement of the sea mills them to yellow salt, mingled with stale crustaceans, the nail clippings of the ocean bed. The sun has a simple journey to make each day, rising from a sea and setting in an ocean.

Or you could take the night train south from the Gare d'Austerlitz, where a mix of diesel and Gauloise smudges the air, underlaid, say the southerners, with a scent of gardenia. The orange- and grey-painted night train, colours of evening and dawn, goes south. It has been marked out for a special journey, and will not be stopping at Lyons. There are other trains, trains from different stations, going to Avignon and Provence. But the Paris to Port Bou is a special train, a train that leaves the capital at night and arrives in the early morning by the sea. It's the train you would take if you were a resistant, escaping into Spain, the train that Jessica, the Communist Mitford, took, and by which Laurie Lee returned to the Civil War. It is always full of soldiers whose shaven heads you'd almost like to

11

stroke, for a dare, and Parisians *en route* to see their families in the south.

Last time I came down it was early July. I shared a compartment with an elderly woman and a thin, ginger-haired girl called Geneviève. She wore platform shoes made of foam rubber, so she walked as on a bouncy castle, which helped for getting in and out of the top bunk while her grandmother slept. She was going to stay with her country cousin for the summer. On the bottom bunk, Geneviève laid out her grandmother, drugged by the heat and her own enormous weight. I was stretched out on my bunk, reading, with my head facing east and feet facing west. She was tall in her platforms and her eyes met mine.

'You're not afraid to travel alone?'

'Afraid?'

She tutted her tongue against her teeth. 'My sister came down here last summer. She was attacked on the train. Me, I'm spending the night with the soldiers next door.'

In the middle of the night, too hot to sleep, I thought I'd go out into the corridor and watch as the train passed through station after empty station, and some people got off, but no-one got on; the train emptied and became lighter as it went south. I twisted the door knob, but Geneviève had locked me and her grandmother in. The compartment was stifling and buzzed with the vibrations from grandmother's chest. Geneviève was with the soldiers, telling them dirty stories about what she and her girlfriends got up to at the ice rink in Lille down by the Eurocentre on a Saturday night.

She crept back in and packed my leather jacket into her suitcase while I slept, emptying the pockets and leaving a pile of receipts and metro tickets at the foot of my bunk. In the morning, a man I recognized, who had been standing out in the corridor all night in a shiny suit and Fred Astaire shoes, drinking whisky from a miniature Evian bottle, came in and sat down with Geneviève and her grandmother. It was five thirty and we had passed Toulouse. He placed himself in between them, so they went up in size as they got further from the corridor and nearer to the window, and began to tell them made-up stories about the war. At least they weren't *his* true stories. They may have been somebody's, but I knew they weren't his. He was the cousin of the butcher in the Rue St Florian who had swallowed a crown in the dentist's chair. He had been caught out in 1942, delivering British airmen and French and German Jews into the hands of the Germans for ten francs a head, and was sent, for his own safety, to a labour camp in Germany. After the war he returned to the village, where people spat at him in the street. In France, post 1945, it was good to have someone to spit at. He still wasn't popular fifty years on, but he had managed to use his notoriety as a basis for a new, post-war personality, even if nobody, not even his own cousin, actually liked him. This was not what he was telling Geneviève and her grandmother.

Out of the carriage window, the train passes, at dawn, pale, wide beaches, fringed by the Sigean marshes, soft violet with green rushes. The grey sky turns silver, then the greyness drains, all last pigment of night departing, to reveal only morning blue from here to Africa. This part of the world is a colour wheel; wherever you find a colour you find its opposite, too. Violets and greens and oranges and greys and blacks and whites. The marshy waters, a birdwatcher's paradise in September and March, suck and lap at the edges of a Moorish fortress, which has one eye on the bay to the north and the other on the Iberian south. For all its fierce posturing, its windswept grimace out to sea, it never saw much action. It's a sort of display model that's been sitting out there on the forecourt of history for seven centuries. Here is where the border used to lie. Queen Amelia, wife of Louis Philippe, kept nudging it south so that Spanish chocolate imports could land in France and be sent up to Paris duty free, without the knowledge of her fiscally scrupulous husband. Pink flamingos stalk among the reeds, prodding at plankton, like park keepers gathering scraps of paper and leaves on pointed canes. In the evening I've seen them stand with the eastern breeze sculpting their feathers to their skulls, gazing west, watching the ghosts of their flamey cousins streak across the sky.

Just north of here is the beach at Gruissan, planted with wooden huts on stilts, made famous in the opening scenes of *Betty Blue*. The original French title was *37.2 degrés*, so that in French it was a fiery red film, and in English a sad blue one. Stefan, a retired Maoist revolutionary, ran a restaurant here at the end of the Seventies, where they served salads and fish with no sauces, and bowls of fresh fruit. An assault on classic French cuisine, he said, is an assault on the state. A colony of Zen monks were living in the huts and went out in rowing boats to catch fish for the restaurant every morning.

Inland lie the Corbières, a slice of spaghetti western country, layered artfully into rural France. At the eastern end, the Cistercian abbey of Fontfroide sits buried in the rock like the skeleton of a prehistoric bird. It was here that St Bernard supped and rested, belched and prayed, before moving inland to smoke out the rebel Cathars.

You pass, but the train does not stop at, the village of Tautavel, where Europe's earliest man is laid out on display – crusted in the earth from 450,000 BC until 1971 when he was dug up to a world where Serge

Gainsbourg was singing 'Je t'aime . . . moi non plus' and the Baader Meinhoff were blowing up shopping centres. They make strong wines here: a red Fitou, and a sweet white wine, Rivesaltes, named after the village from which all traces of a former concentration camp have smoothly been erased. A man who makes pigments lives in Tautavel. Painters from as far away as Nice and Barcelona pay him twice-yearly visits and come away with little phials of colour, condensed down to something so powerful you could spill a droplet in a summer storm and the sea would be awash with that colour from here to Africa. It's a country of painters and cowboys. Just inland from Narbonne, where the train stops for half an hour, is a village where you can buy Bob Blooming saddles and saddle soap and bridles from a man who, in his head, lives in the American Far West. He teaches cowboy-style riding: how to bring your horse to an instant standstill from a flat-out gallop. There is no practical application for this skill, unless you have it in mind to go for gallops on the British Airways runway at Perpignan airport, or impress girls at the beach.

Sometimes, especially in the valley of the Corbières, where the stone is gaunt and the vegetation dry as an unseasoned saddle, you come round a corner to discover, almost to your surprise, not a hacienda or a cattle ranch, but a lush vineyard and an eighteenth-century villa. You could leap from the train with your luggage and tramp past the Cistercian abbey, buy paint from the pigment man in Tautavel and make your way on up the iron-red road to the Château de Puig. Madame Estère would brush you down and find you lodgings, and if you were beautiful and talented and male, she might even show your work.

Madame Estère's husband owns the vineyard. She is a generous patron of contemporary art, and on the

15

opening evening of their exhibitions they serve their own fragrant vintage, with labels designed by a north African artist from Nice. Last summer the staff of Air Inter went on strike on the day of the opening, and all the Parisian gallery owners and critics were grounded. Only the locals turned up, and the odd dealer from Nice, Barcelona and Toulouse. There was a high wind, and I stood at the window on the first floor while they served drinks outside, watching the tramontane, which blows from the north, sculpt the ladies' skirts round their thighs as the wine grew choppy inside their glasses. At dinner, under the pergola, I sat next to a famous English writer's fragile widow, so fragile she might have been reconstituted from ash, who complained about the loud-mouthed lover of a former Lagerfeld model across the table. The former model was only in her forties, but she had platinum white hair and was wearing trainers and a crushed-silk skirt down to her ankles, bunched about her waist. Even beautiful women no longer knew how to dress. Especially beautiful women, added a woman next to her. The loud-mouthed lover had painted a picture called *Woman Met in Martinique, Who Left Me*, and was looking for his cigarette lighter under the table for an hour. There was a crushed car by César in the fore-court. The painter of honour was a sad American married to a beautiful, rich and efficient French-woman. He'd almost died three years previously, and was planning to leave his wife of twenty years for the doctor who had cured him, who was not beautiful, nor rich, though she was efficient at curing bone cancer. He poured these secrets into my ear throughout the meal, so everyone thought it must be me he was planning to run off with. He kept saying, 'She's so hot! Boy, is she hot!'

All this just behind the fold in the hill where the

train goes past. The guidebooks say it is a landscape full of surprises. Out of the corridor window, the Canigou appears, stately, outlined against the thin grey sky at dawn, a sail, the skirt of a ball gown caught in a moment of grace. Snow caps the summit from October to May, catching a few minutes of peachy light every morning. The sun sets behind it in the evening. An insurance company tried to buy the mountain once, because they'd heard that Virgil had said it was the most beautiful mountain in the world, but no-one could work out who to buy it from. So the insurance company bought a mountain in the Alps instead. That's the difference between the Pyrenees and the Alps: you can buy the Alps.

Don't miss the recorded voice saying, '*Perpignan, ici Perpignan.*' It rolls and chimes; there are bells and the white flutter of an agitated sea in her diction. She is waking you with a caress and a catch in her throat. It is a voice that makes you feel hopeful for small things. Welcome to Perpignan. Welcome to Catalunia. Disembarkation takes place here. Do not forget your luggage in the train. Passengers slam back the doors, step out and stretch their creases, bladders full, skin tight, eyes strained. The soldiers, elastic because they are young, swing their bags into the corridor and uncrumple their cigarettes.

Even before the train stops, we dissolve and separate, night travellers who have all dreamed the same dream, just this once. Already we are looking for eyes that are looking for us, for friends who will grasp our bags and lead us away to our various, individual destinations. Sometimes it is good not to be met off a train, to carry on dreaming, prolonging the night state so that the new place seems like a continuation of the dream, from which fellow travellers have woken before you.

The Station

Perpignan railway station – the most beautiful station in the world. Forget Grand Central, St Pancras, Austerlitz or the Gare d'Orsay. It is the last main station in France; but the track carries on beyond, world without end. Look up to see the ceiling, painted in orange psychedelic swirls, a meditation on the direness of French wallpaper – wallpaper always goes on the ceiling in France, and since we do not have eyes in the top of our heads the ceiling is probably the best place for it. Salvador Dali declared that Perpignan had the most beautiful railway station in the world, not only that, but that Perpignan *was* the centre of the world. Now there's a statue of him on the forecourt, in bronze. It is a fine illustration of how your worst jokes are always the ones people remember.

When you get off the train, look for the timetable for the little green bus – the green of the wrapper for the triangle-shaped chocolate in the Quality Street box – which is in the first coach bay, opposite the Café de la Gare. They leave once an hour. You can wait in the Café de la Gare. You can get croissants at any time of day. They respect the fact that, if you've come this far, it might be any time of day for you. Last time I had just ordered a coffee, too hot to drink, when the coach arrived. I'd left my rucksack with a man who was also waiting to go to the village. His brother was dangerously ill, he said. It was the only thing that would bring him back here. They are racist bigots, the Catalans, he said. They think this is a paradise on earth, and that if it's paradise on earth then they must be gods. They are vain and introverted. I wondered whether he meant they were vain and introverted to think themselves gods, or whether, being godlike, vanity and introversion were two of their characteristics. He put my rucksack on the coach and waved to me through the café window. I put down my coffee cup and ran. I held out my thirteen francs to the driver, but he waved me back. 'Go and drink your coffee,' he said. 'We are not savages here.'

The green bus will take you to the village in anything from twenty-five minutes to an hour. Try not to look at the shopping centres on the outskirts of Perpignan, and comfort yourself with the thought that they will all fall down in ten years anyway. When the bus gets to the spa town, where there is a hint of Vichy in the water, it takes a back road and sets down rheumatic sufferers at the entrance to the thermal baths. They leave their bags at the gate for the porter and walk slowly, arm in arm, past the rhododendrons and the plumbago, eager to be soothed and cured, but unable to walk at more than a careful picking pace. Many of them have their treatment paid for by the state, particularly retired soldiers and their wives. It's cheaper and more effective than free prescriptions. A lot of them register to vote down here, being regulars, which helps the National Front and enrages the local Left. The National Front hugs the coast, and the communists stand their ground inland, with their backs to the mountains.

Here the autoroute crosses the southernmost valley in France, then burns on and away, as motorways always do, this one up and over into Spain. Cars heading into Spain cross the border as though on the back of some great white bird, sweeping down into the flat land west of the fishing ports of the Costa Brava. Lorries from Amsterdam, caravans from Cologne, Mini Travellers, packed to the last square, gasping inch with holiday luggage, plunge on, away, up and over, past the idling border guards, the sporadically alert Guardia Civil, stopping for breaks at service stations, the coffee getting stronger, the meat in the sandwiches saltier and the tobacco in the cigarettes rougher and more pungent as they go. But if you are arriving by car, on the autoroute or Via Domitia, this is where you leave it, with the sudden winded feeling you get when you leave a motorway, as though you had just jumped from a moving train. You have come so far it is tempting to carry on, to follow the swallow-call of the south, to disregard this possibly unimportant place to which you have travelled all these hundreds of miles for your holiday blind date, for holidays in new places are blind dates with a landscape, a town, a temporary lodging, a place where the sun sets differently from home.

You pay your toll at the little window, and the song of the girl's voice as she wishes you good evening, and even the green resin smell of the vegetation expelling its evening heat, tell you your journey has brought you where you wanted to go. As you idle in the lay-by, studying the directions to your final destination, you will see, if you look up at the silhouette of the dark green hills against the sky, the white, soaring bridge high-stepping over the final valley. Thirteen men were killed at one blow when a stick of misplaced dynamite went off while it was being built. A plaque sunk into the cement commemorates their death. Just south of here is where Hannibal drove his army and his elephants through a cleft in the hills, a border town now. On one side of the street you pay for your cheap leatherware and Spanish lace in pesetas, and on the other you can buy duty-free Gauloises and cognac in francs.

Painters have always been drawn here. Matisse and the Fauves painted the glossy fishing barques at Collioure against a background of pink stone and childish blue jiggles of water. Picasso came with Braque in 1911 and spent three summers here. Their letters to friends and dealers back in Paris mention that they had discovered a beautiful place. But they painted it out of all recognition, twisting its features and redrawing its contours with wilful strokes of the brush. Picasso's women had to be sure of their beauty; how else could they have stood being made to look like queens in a lunatic set of playing cards? Here was a landscape similarly assured.

Pause at the roundabout. Fold away the map. The river valley spreads before you in soft geometric shapes, a canvas from Claude Lorrain. The road runs straight from here, lined with a row of plane trees – *platanes* – on the river side. There used to be a parallel line of plane trees on the other side of the road, and the two joined branches in the middle, forming a canopy beneath which people rode into town under a full day's sun. They cut down one side in the 1960s because the tree cover was so dense that people kept crashing into each other in the midday dark.

People say this is all that's left of Arcadia, but there are no mythological figures, no cavorting fauns or maidens swaddled in young white fat reclining by pools. A farmer walks through the vines, squeezing the new grapes thoughtfully and watching the pull of the western wind on the night clouds as they are tugged away and up towards the highest peaks. Adolescents lean against their *motocyclettes* on the dirt track that leads down to the lake where they will swim, do their homework, eat burgers from the café or make love behind it. When we drive back up the valley from the beach, or even sometimes from Montpellier or Toulouse, Luc says, 'Look at me, stealing back like a guilty husband,' as though he'd committed an infidelity just by leaving home.

Devil's Bridge

Get off the bus. Cross the Devil's Bridge. The world authority on devil's bridges, Gaspard Dupont, lives in the village. He had a job in computers, went off to Africa with it, came back without it and didn't move from the counter of the Café Central for the next three years. His eye sockets grew slack as his eyes shrank, preserved at half volume in pastis, into the back of his head. His cheeks grew sprigs of purple capillaries, which fanned out over his face like alpine plants on a rockery.

Gaspard was walking home one summer night after a drinking bout with the insurance broker, Maurice. Maurice had a broken heart for which no solace could be found, no restitution made. He took Gaspard to the bridge, shook his hand and said, '*Adieu*; this is where it ends.' But there must have been a protection plan somewhere with Maurice's name on it. When he tried to launch himself into the air he found the muscles in his legs were swamped with liquid. He sagged, defeated, to the ground at Gaspard's feet, and soon fell into a restoring slumber. Alone on the Devil's Bridge under a full summer moon, Gaspard experienced a moment of quiet epiphany and fell in love with the stones.

He measured and paced it, and photographed it from

23

down by the river and up the top of the hill. Then he discovered that this Devil's Bridge was not the only one. It had cousins and relations all over Europe. One evening he sat down at my table on the café terrace, looked me steadily in the eye and said, 'Kirk–by Lons–dale.' 'Yes,' I said, I knew it quite well. I had jumped off it as a teenager. Someone else had jumped off it that summer and been killed. He was delighted. It was as though, for him, all other devil's bridges were virtual. My affirmation of its existence at some point in the past brought that virtuality forward a little, and we both sat there at the café table, watching it nudge into focus in our imagination, he looking forward at it, as something new, and I looking back at it, as something old, once known.

There are three bridges over the river as you come into the village. The Devil's Bridge, on your left, is for pedestrians only. It's called the Devil's Bridge because legend says the devil built it and invoiced the village for the soul of whoever should cross it first. The villagers sent a cat, but the devil was not deceived. It's an unsatisfactory story, because it doesn't say who was sent in place of the cat. To your right is the old railway bridge, and the middle bridge for the D115, which joins up with a roundabout. Here they sometimes build roundabouts just in case they need them later on, even though there are no roads to feed into them yet, and no plans for any. Town planning becomes a giant exercise in joining up the dots. The big house on the left by the fruit shop with the surreally cheap prices – twenty avocados for five francs! thirty kiwis for ten! – is where Picasso stayed during his first summer in the village in 1911. A bit further on up the valley is a fourth bridge, made of metal, which used to carry the railway line back across the river. It is known as 'La Tour Eiffel: reclining'.

Car drivers take the last exit off the first roundabout, the last exit off the second roundabout, the first exit off the third roundabout and then the second right at a sign for the car park. The new road, Acacia Avenue du Midi, sweeps past the fire station and up to the equestrian centre, where ten or eleven horses mooch and a few lone rangers sit around under a beautiful grass-hut construction, lamenting the departure of the cowboys for the Far West Club near Tautavel. The town is built in concentric circles around a fountain in a square. Though it is technically a town, and in Italy would be called a city, the locals always call it '*le village*'. To say 'the village' is like calling a woman by her maiden name because you knew her before she married someone you didn't like. The fountain head is a carved stone lion, which, when the town was Spanish, used to look south towards Spain. During the seventeenth century, when it became French, they took the lion's head off and turned it to face France. One year, during the *feria*, there was a fight over it, and a group of men from Barcelona tried to wrench it round again. The manager of the pizzeria found it in the gutter on the Monday morning and took it to the *mairie* – the town hall – where it now sits in the in-tray of an idle councillor.

The house is built into the sixteenth-century ramparts and is two minutes on foot from the fountain. Park in the top corner of the car park and walk through the little stone arch, past the round fortress tower where washing hangs in place of flags. A group of teenagers sit smoking and kissing on the stone wall at the foot of the tower. In France, smoking and kissing have never been seen as antithetical, and both activities tend to be embarked on young. In a niche in the outer wall of the house opposite, a stone cat sits watching. No. 11 is the last house on the right, the one with the bulge in the wall and the double coach doors.

The woman next door sits outside because there is nowhere to sit inside her house, not because she is curious or waiting for anyone. She will smile at you as you pass her door and bare the gaps where her teeth should be. She went to Luc last year saying she'd lost her dentures; he made her a new set. She went back a week later and said she had lost them, too. They decided between them that the reason she kept losing them was because she didn't really want any teeth. There were no words she particularly wanted to say that couldn't be said without them.

The key is in an envelope pinned to the door. It's a tiny modern Yale key and it fits the top lock. There is a key from a completely different kingdom that fits the bottom lock, but it's so big it's kept in a tin bucket under the sink. Objects have a way of finding their proper places that isn't very different from the way people or animals find places to settle into – arbitrary and unaccountable, but, if you're lucky, just right. Pull the door sharply towards you, turn the key twice to the left, push with your knee and, at the same time, turn the huge metal ring which once would have been used for tethering your horse or mule. Hang the key on the hook just inside the door. If you lose it there is a spare behind the bar at the café under the plane trees.

The House

The house was built in the sixteenth century, according to the documents in the *mairie*, and in structure, at least, it's a typical village house, on three floors, with the living accommodation on the first and second floors, and car or animals at ground level. The terrace on the first floor at the back is what estate agents call a selling point. At the moment it overlooks the old cobbled piggery, where strange, unauthorized things grow up between the stones, but if extended out to cover that dingy space, gaining another fifteen feet, it would be quite an addition to the house. Year after year, though, for lack of money, it remains the same, rather scruffy perfect patch of light, with a purple bougainvillea growing up one wall and a pink bougainvillea growing up the other. People come and shake their heads and say, 'That'll never take,' or, 'That'll dry out,' and 'I'll take my hat off to you if that survives!' Occasionally, freak conditions bring about a rare coincidence of colours in bloom. In the middle of May, like two eyebrow-raisingly ill-matched lovers at a ball, pretty blue plumbago and orange California poppies, the very colour of pollen, appear side by side, unannounced. The rich dirty-golden poppies, for all the brazenness of their flowers, are delicate, and their fragile stems will easily break unless you sow them so thick they stand in a dense frondy thicket. Plumbago has an unusual characteristic: just as its name doesn't match its shape, its flowers don't match its foliage, either in shade or form, so that it's never quite as beautiful as it should be. Its woody stems bear cold blue flowers with tiny forget-me-not petals, hesitant and pale.

Water the plants before breakfast, before the sun hits the back wall. You can really only have breakfast out there without a shade if you get up earlier than you probably want to on holiday, otherwise you'll find yourself staggering back inside with sunstroke, singing top Cs in your head. Better to lie in bed and wait until the shadow burns off the sheets and the sun steals through your eyelashes and lights up the inside of your head, draping your inner eyelids with phosphorescent coral strands. Then you can open the windows wide and lean out and shake yourself gently awake. In summer your eyes are filled first with the light and the mountain and the sky, and then, as their focus gradually sharpens and is able to register smaller things, the lines of the houses clear. A bird appears on the wall opposite, the trees grow branches and individual leaves, hesitant flowers unfold on the wall and in the pots below, and an insect works its way down a beautifully drawn line, a fibre of colour leading inwards to the stamen and a grain of smutty pollen.

At least that's how it seems to me, with my English eyes and the English words I have to describe what I see. The French language went through the equivalent of colonic irrigation in the 1960s, when Robbe-Grillet announced that 'any attempt to endow the physical world with emotion is a step towards the illicit belief in God'. Once he described the exact dimensions of a window, supplying detail upon grinding detail, ignoring the fabulous blue view beyond. Maybe he deliberately lived somewhere where you wouldn't want to look beyond the window frame, just in case one morning he found his heart pounding and gods sliding down greasy poles from heaven to frolic below. I know a flower can't be hesitant, because it doesn't have a consciousness. I know a mountain shouldn't loom majestically, it's not a God or a prophet or a dictator. I know looming majestically is a cliché. But there has to be something between that and flatly stating its shape and measurements. Often an aeroplane crosses the mountain here on its way to Barcelona, soundless, scarcely visible, betrayed, as it steals over the border, by its long white tail, soft as a rabbit's, but drawn out in time, what Stefan calls *un moment Godard*. Stefan's officially with Robbe-Grillet when it comes to descriptive language; but he knows that when he rings me in the quiet early afternoon and says, 'Look out of the window, *ma belle*, it's a *moment Godard*,' the words exhale a puff of softest innuendo.

Over the terrace wall, the backs of the houses of the Rue des Commerçants describe a chaotic D, like an amphitheatre whose back central stage is this little terrace. It wiggles, up along and up, from the Place de la République to the Place de la Liberté. The Rue des Commerçants is cobbled and treacherous, with water gushing along the gutters on either side. You can shake hands with your neighbour opposite without leaving your front room. The houses are tall, very tall, but all of different heights, creating a crenellated kind of effect, with mountain views for some. Each house, so grim and sheer seen from the sunless well of the Rue des Commerçants, bursts out onto the gardens, which are their shared, delicious secret. It is as though, backstage, away from public view, every idiosyncrasy of colour and shape has been indulged. Each house looks like a children's dressing-up trunk that has been plundered, contents spilling out into the sun.

The ground floor is empty. You can hang your washing out in the piggery. There is a tiny water closet, a pile of wood for the stove in winter, a wine store and a back room full of gummed-up paint pots. The iron banister rail has a few sharp bits; don't grip it too tight or it will tear shreds out of your palms.

On the first floor there's the terrace and a pair of *portes-fenêtres* through which to step out onto it from the sitting room – wooden floor; one table; one sofa; two cane chairs from the market in Figueras; one etching of a shepherd sitting on the grass, looking at Hillsborough House; one painting by Luc, who painted nothing else in this house. Small toilet with a weak flush. Kitchen – one Welsh dresser, with fragile panes of glass; cooker new; fridge new. Telephone numbers and addresses for doctors and dentists, and emergency numbers, are on the sheet of paper stuck on the side of the dresser. In the corner, for winter, there's a cast-iron stove with zinc pipes leading to the chimney. There's cutlery in the drawers, pans hanging from the wall, plates and cooking equipment in the dresser, napkins and tablecloths in one drawer; pegs, screwdrivers, tape, pliers, possibly corkscrews, drawing pins, curtain hooks, Polyfilla in a tube, superglue and shoe polish in the other. I like the way you discover day by day, when you move into somewhere new, what you really need in life, what the bare necessities really are.

The staircase winds up from the kitchen to the second floor. On your left, at the front of the house, overlooking the street, so you can exchange vowel sounds with the woman next door by hanging out of the window, and catch a glimpse of the top of the mountain if you hang out dangerously far, is the smaller yellow bedroom with grey doors. All the floors are wooden, and make a lot of noise unless you tread lightly as you go. Walk down the short corridor to the main bedroom, where the sun wakes you if you choose not to close the flaking shutters before you go to sleep. White walls, blue window, the same view as the terrace. The house opposite was bought by one of the four village pharmacists, the one who'll write you out prescriptions in his room above the shop so that, if you are a tourist and uninsured, you can avoid a doctor's bill by going straight to him. Beyond, with gardens spreading up the sides of the hills, is the house where Picasso lived in his later summers, with forty-two windows, each with a painted pair of grey-blue shutters. From the same window you can see the house Le Corbusier's partner built for his own retirement; slim, white, rectangular, like a video cassette slid into the mountainside. From this height you can see more of the southern hills, though not the lakes that lie behind, and the particular mountain that leads you up over the Route des Evadés into Spain. Every eleventh of November the mayor follows it up to the border with his entourage and some of the surviving Spaniards who left Spain under Franco, to sing a republican hymn around a stone which says, 'By this path, 500,000 Spaniards escaped from the Falangists between 1937 and 1939'. And the last building on the road before Spain is the farm where Luc sits rolling his cigarettes hour after hour and looking up in silence into the leaves of a tree. Luc felt well placed, living on a path called the Route des Evadés, along which people had escaped in both directions – Spaniards, and later Jews and other enemies of the Third Reich. Whenever I got restless and felt the need to go off for a while and see the world, he would point up the hill to the border and say, 'It's that way.' In 1959 Picasso visited the village, and Luc's father took him up there to look out over Spain. Picasso had planned to build

31

his Chapelle de la Paix up there, so the farm would have become a sandwich shop for pilgrims, but according to Luc's father, he spat on the ground when he realized that from the top of the hill you could see not only the whole of the sweep of hills and the plain as far as the bay of Cadaqués, but also the point of land on which Dali had built his home at Port Lligat. Picasso built his Chapelle de la Paix in much-visited Saint-Paul de Vence instead, where, as Luc points out, they never get a moment's peace.

This is the theatre of my life, a little hidden-away theatre where the dramas are domestic, and entrances and exits are marked by nothing more dramatic, usually, than the closing of a door, the clasping at night of a pair of shutters, someone looking for a lost toy in a garden, finding it and stepping back indoors again. A child in the house to the left with the garden plays the piano in that tense, unsure way children do. Her mother jogs every morning with the chemist's wife. They are both beautifully tanned and sleek. They run along the edge of the river and down through the peach orchard, past the horses and through the car park, their light trainer fall pattering through the dreams of the travellers sleeping in camper vans parked up on the verge. They come home and drink lemonade in the garden, eat swedish crackers from the health-food shop and talk about their children while, in late summer, heavy fruit falls into the soft grass. But from here you can never catch what they are saying, so I don't really know if it is the little girl or one of her brothers who plays Scarlatti with ill humour, and sometimes Chopin with reluctant, halting tenderness.

The Village

It was a Roman town, then a flourishing market town; it was Spanish for a while, then French for a while. In the nineteenth century the vine crop failed, so they planted peach and cherry trees instead. Although the people are small, they planted normal-sized fruit trees, whose fruit they collected by climbing up a ladder with a basket. Then dwarf varieties were planted in Provence, where they are much more organized. There they don't need ladders or baskets to collect their crop, so their labour costs are lower and their prices cheaper. But the village is still famous for producing the first cherries of the year, traditionally sent to the president's table in the second week of May. I like to think of his face lighting up after breakfast at the start of a busy day, as Mme La Présidente says chirpily, 'Cherries tonight, *chéri!*'

Most of the 8,000 inhabitants don't live in the old town, but in the *lotissements* – housing estates – outside. The old town coils round the square, with the lion fountain and friendly restaurants, a tall hive of inter-locking streets which barely see the light except at midday. Old people live in the old houses, for the most part. Old women sit outside their houses all day, shooing dogs. An English friend calls the road where the house is 'Dog Alley'.

The church is in the middle of the hive, the madonna statuette crouched in a niche above the dusky altar. It's built in honey sandstone, with pink brick tiles. From the front entrance it looks eleventh-century. Great wooden doors open into a paved circus. Inside it's nineteenth-century, hideous and cold. Only an old person could feel happy there. Perhaps even only a dead one.

Funerals are held at one o'clock. While everyone is having lunch a hearse draws up. You see the sons and daughters of the deceased climbing out of cars with Paris number plates in the late morning, and even catching a bite to eat in the restaurant where the travelling salesmen go. Sometimes there will be a sibling left in town, who has never travelled further than the Pont du Diable, and they walk uneasily side by side behind the coffin, their children eyeing each other up, half scornful, half intrigued. Later there will be feuds about the inheritance. The family and the women of the town attend the service, while the men, sometimes up to 200 of them, as in the case of the funeral of Luc's mother — Miss Béziers, 1937 — stand around outside and smoke and talk about the dead. It's a restful scene, these men gathered in the church square. There's a peace about them that draws the unincluded. They look protective, as though you would be safe in their midst; they form groups which you could read, if you had the knowledge, for friendship, for village history, for lives shared. It would be nice to glide among them, invisible, and hear what they said.

Walking through the narrow streets of the old town you are within touching distance of people eating inside their kitchens — always meat of some kind, or fish. The smell of fish as you round a corner can be so strong and aromatic that the walls start to flicker and you look up and see the hulls of little boats bobbing over your head. In summer you can feel the chill coming off sunless kitchen tiles. The interiors of these houses are brown, cold, stone. The conversations are always loud and vivacious. There is often a Spanish TV channel to be shouted over. By one o'clock everything has been cleared away and the old couples climb into their beds and sleep.

Widows eat frugally alone, then go out and sit outside the *mairie* in their floral-print housecoats and talk. They sit side by side on a bench reserved for them, and nod at the young world passing by on foot. One day Luc saw one of his patients, a friend of his deceased mother, sitting there on the bench. There was a space beside her, so he sat down and asked her how she was getting on with her dentures. Very well, she replied; she was very happy. She smiled and sat back, watching the world. Since she seemed content for him to be there, Luc sat on beside her, smiling slightly, too, sighing unconsciously when she sighed, nodding off when she did. Afterwards I said, 'I saw you on the bench with the old ladies.' He said thoughtfully, 'You know, for once in my life I felt completely well with the world.'

When he says something like that I feel the terror of growing old and dying in a foreign place. In the daytime it seems like a glorious choice, existential in its arbitrariness. While my contemporaries are back in London, living lives between the office and their homes, in terraces of houses, on tubes, in long lines of things, I've attached myself to this landscape, like a bird whose homing system has thrown up a weirdly mutated set of instructions. But it's an unnerving freedom, and the thought that the exercising of it could take up the rest of my life strikes me in the night. No-one knows anything about me, except that I am from somewhere else. No-one knows about my childhood, or has ever asked me about where I studied or lived before. No-one interprets my accent, or who I know, or who I went to school with, or what job I do, or my post-code in London, or any of the other things that give you an identity, even if it's a false one, when you are among your own. Whenever I go back to London I feel naked, the way people can read so much about you that you don't even know you're displaying. Here, I am the sum of my spoken words, the way I walk down the street, of accumulated present moments that might one day stack up high enough for a pattern to emerge. Nothing I have done before I came here has any weight. They accept me without question, on condition I shed my past.

The Boulevard

The Romans made an irrigation system to bring water down from the border hills into the town for their gardens. Thinking of the Romans as gardeners makes you want to discover their gardening literature. Was it Virgil who wrote about gardens and husbandry? Or Ovid? Did Romans take their holidays in places like this? Virgil must have, if he wrote about the mountain, arriving by boat, having sailed from somewhere like Genoa across the Mediterranean bay to land . . . where? On one of the flat beaches of Sigean? Or Empurda, a Roman settlement only a few hours from here by a slow means of transport, itself built on the remains of a Greek town by the sea. Stefan says ruins always look best beside the sea.

I don't know what the Romans did here, or when; nobody seems to, but they built, that's for certain, and they gardened. A garden is a luxury in a walled town. Walking under the Devil's Bridge and along the banks of the river, where it spills over into the fields, you can see the village allotments, where most people grow their vegetables and flowers. The water comes down the mountain, through stone gullies, canals and underground channels, till it splashes down behind the ironmonger's shop and then along the gutters, sluicing, cleaning and disturbing the air even on the stillest day.

Cunning villagers creep out at dawn, when there is a drought, to divert water onto their land with fallen rocks and stones.

You emerge from the sluiced cobbled alleys onto the tarmacked boulevard which runs along three sides of the town. A boulevard is a nineteenth-century invention. The outlines for it here must have been clear; it runs from the Porte de France, links up with the Porte d'Espagne, past the café, and right up to the Place de la Liberté – renamed after the war. Here is Maillol's war memorial, a mother slumped in grief, her stone hands heavy in her unwarmed lap. On 1 May hundreds of villagers gather here in their shirtsleeves to sing the 'Internationale', with a fist in the air. And on your right is the stone washing house, where women who don't have a washing machine and consider it too late in life to get used to the launderette, still come to plunge their laundry into freezing mountain water.

Although the village is busy with visitors from late spring until the end of summer, it is not a place that dies in winter. Young people often stay and make their lives here, opening cafés or wine shops, or going into business. In the old town centre alone there are three insurance brokers, four banks, two supermarkets, three ironmongers, six *épiceries*, a *fromagerie*, two wine cellars – you can fill up the plastic vats in the cellar with good vin de pays for nine francs a litre – five butchers, nine *boulangeries*, five hairdressers, three florists, seven doctors, eight dentists, twelve dress shops and three newsagents.

The Maison de la Presse, the large newsagent a couple of doors down from the Museum of Modern Art, is regarded with suspicion, a corruption of the local, rather modest gene pool. It used to be dark and poky, like the other two, and sell sweets, tobacco, papers and lottery tickets. Then, it is said, the owners

38

– originally from Paris – won the lottery themselves. They bought up the buildings on either side, and their shop is now bigger than the average WH Smith. You can buy John Grisham and Jeffrey Archer, and magazines in every European language. Tourists queue for their copy of the *Daily Telegraph* or the *Frankfurter Allgemeine*. Schoolchildren buy confectionery with artificial colourings and Spice Girl transfers to stick on their upper arms. Japanese watches and carriage clocks are displayed in padlocked glass cases. They sell Basildon Bond, Queen's Velvet and Parker pens.

The owner, Madame Arnoux, is small and dark, with her hair in a chignon and the same round, brown eyes as her namesake in Flaubert's *L'Education sentimentale*. She is a proud *commerçante*. Her husband is a funereal man with a chalky face. I have a disturbing recurrent image of him standing looking in the bathroom mirror, gripping the edge of the basin as she calls to him from the bedroom, reminding him of the chores of the day ahead. And yet I may be wrong, because her eyes are warm, the colour of oxtail soup, and it must be good to wake up to a fine pair of eyes that are never cold. Her speech is one long, hyphenated sentence of greeting, consolation, price-naming and scolding, from eight till eight. She seems to run on sherbert, fizzing *Thatcherisme* with her fast, till-tapping fingers and her reprimanding cries to the staff: 'No, Gaston, the *Guardian* for Mr Herbert, not *The Times*, thirteen francs, there you are, your change, sir, thank you, Gauloises Rouges, certainly, eleven francs, lucky number, never mind, not today, another one.' She knows what everybody smokes, and people feel comfortable buying cigarettes from her. The more people smoke, the happier she is. 'Relax!' she cries, as she unwraps another wadge of tobacco. 'Monsieur, enjoy your pipe!' When I go in to buy Luc's cigarette papers she tries to persuade me to take the ones with gummed edges, but he won't have them. He says the gum is unnecessary, that you just have to use the right amount of spit. 'You know what that man's motto is?' she cries. '"Why be straightforward when you could be *compliqué*?"'

On Saturday mornings the boulevard becomes a market place. You can buy organic vegetables, goat's cheese, honey, fish, oysters, wine, buttons, pegs, screws, flowers, plants, lace, fabrics, spices, soaps, chickens, dried salt cod, olives, olive oil, bread, paella, terrine, prunes and salami. On Monday and Tuesday mornings it is full of parked lorries unloading into shops. On Wednesday it is taken over by children and teenagers who have the afternoon off from school. They are meant to spend it doing improving things, like learning another language or having riding lessons or painting at the Museum's art class, but most of them just smoke and flirt and walk the boulevard.

Every evening, before dinner and after work, the grown men walk the boulevard, too. Luc comes out of his dental surgery at seven and stands with his dog, his hands in his pockets, nodding at people he knows. He rolls a cigarette, then sets off along the boulevard, under the plane trees. The dog follows. In spring, after the plane trees have flowered, they walk in a cloud of fairy's cotton, sometimes sneezing. At the junction of the boulevard and the Rue Costète he is joined by Monsieur Montiel, the pharmacist.

I am standing outside the grocer's looking at vegetables laid out in baskets, feeling odd because I have just been writing about the mining town in South Yorkshire where I lived as a child, and I feel as though someone has sat on the remote control and accidentally flicked me into this busy early evening scene of warm stones, fluttering awnings and flowers. Stefan comes by on his bicycle, wearing shorts and a clean T-shirt, with his tennis racquet strapped to his back. He stops and talks to me, but quickly: he has seen Luc out of the corner of his eye and will move off again before he draws near. He comments, with a mixture of crudeness and grace, that since the election the pharmacist, now a town councillor, has a new spring in a part of his anatomy which is not his feet. Stefan does not walk the boulevard because he runs and cycles everywhere, and he condemns it, anyway, as a bourgeois way of laying claim to property and space. There are many foreigners living here and in the outlying villages between the mountains and the sea, and still more Parisians. The locals say of outsiders, '*Ils ne sont pas d'ici*' – they're not from here. Monsieur Montiel and Luc are definitely '*d'ici*'. Walking the boulevard proves it. Stefan, who is from Normandy, laughs and says, '*Si je suis ici, je suis d'ici*'. If I'm here, I belong here.

Outside the Café du Sport they pause. If you are walking the boulevard you can choose to stop and talk to people walking on the pavements or doing their shopping, but you may not interrupt someone who is walking the boulevard unless you are doing it yourself. That's the etiquette. They talk briefly with the man who lives in the house opposite mine, who has a face which, from a distance, looks as though a grenade had exploded across the street and pitted it with scars. In fact, what look like indentations at twenty metres are actually age spots, like shading on a map for points of interest. He has a brother who follows him around all day, from one café to the next, like a child blown up to giant size in a cartoon – adult, but with the features of a ten-year-old. The brother got lost during the bull chase in Pamplona one year and turned up in a police station in Buenos Aires. It is the big mystery of his life, but the great discovery of his life was when Luc cured

41

his teeth-grinding, and with it his migraines, by giving him a box of wooden toothpicks, with instructions to chew one every three hours. Sometimes he and his brother will toss their coins onto the table top and join the walk.

The dog, a black shaggy mountain breed, jiggles and pushes between the newcomers to get back to Luc's side. They stop again outside the Museum of Modern Art. If Luc and his uncle are on speaking terms, he'll join them, too. Outside the dress shop they stop again and chat with Gigi and her assistant, who are locking up and sighing about slack business, or about a woman who wore a dress for a party and returned it, soiled, demanding her money back. The florist rushes out with a delivery for Gigi from her lover in Nîmes. She looks at him coldly because he was caught out last year making anonymous phone calls to her home in the night, heavy breathing and mewing down the line. When, to his disappointment, she failed to identify him, he began sending her anonymous bunches of flowers, then potted plants, sprays of pampas grass, fleshy orchids and, finally reaching the outer limits of his range, paper poppies, plastic tulips, cacti and palms. She got her lover, a famous barrister, to write him a warning letter, and he stopped. Now the barrister gets a thrill from ringing him up at odd times of the day and getting him to take flowers over to Gigi, dictating delicately erotic messages down the phone.

Etienne, who runs the African art shop, waves and goes to order a lemonade. He is from Paris and doesn't walk the boulevard. He'll sit with Anna, the over-worked English teacher with a long white ponytail and a Catalan boyfriend who treats her, as she says, in the old-fashioned way, for which one day he may end up in prison. He is one of a group of men in their forties whose muscular bodies are starting to sag and their gambling debts to add up. They are waiting for their parents to die. Their fathers will die first. When their mothers die, they will weep and drink for a few days, then use the money to set up *brocantes* – second-hand furniture shops – which will fail. Sometimes Anna drinks a slow, cold gin in the early evening and reads a letter from her grown-up daughter in Ashford, England, with the words of her last lesson still ringing in her ears – 'A dolphin can laugh, a dolphin can swim, a dolphin can dive and a dolphin can *sing*!' – Or, if it had been the baccalauréat class, 'Did Jane enjoy "coming off" heroin? What is the meaning of the phrase "cold turkey"?' I stood in for Anna once when she was ill. The text book was so depressing I felt glad to have learned French at a school that made you translate phrases like 'Madame Aimant's cat is a secretive tabby with nine lives'.

The café owner, Astrou, shakes his cloth as the *boulevardiers* pass. Luc's dog walks proudly, like a new recruit. The talk is of the dead and the dying, of horses and painting, of a failed crop, a failed marriage, of local politics, of taxes and feuds. When they draw level with the Salle de Spectacle, they turn. Luc's dog turns first, like a Girl Guide at the front of a parade, a touch too eager to be part of things. They come back past the café, and will repeat the walk, maybe once more, maybe twice, till conversation runs dry or they get thirsty.

I'm still standing by the vegetable baskets. My eyes are on Luc, bewitched by his slow walk, like a dancer's, his tongue flicking out to lick the edge of his roll-up, his strong brown hands gesturing excitedly, giving him away, while the rest of his body is schooled and graceful as an athlete's, and I think I can't leave, I love it here, and I cannot imagine a time when I won't know him more intimately than anyone in the world, and be the one his eyes graze over as he passes, and winks at, and tosses his car keys to as I pull a face to show my shopping is heavy. I'll bring the car round to the café and wait for him there.

The Dress Shop

Luc had made it quite clear, without actually stating it, that he had been the sexual sensation of Gigi's life, and she had lived with many men, including the one who was now married to the Lagerfeld model, and who had painted the picture called *Woman Met in Martinique, Who Left Me*. Now she was well into her fifties and enjoying her late summer beauty. When Luc met me she passed some scathing comments, then gave up and merely stipulated that if he was going to insist on going out with me she should get to dress me. Errors of taste could be kept to a minimum in the clothes department, at least.

All my best clothes came from Gigi's shop. I didn't like the way she looked at me, but I liked the way she dressed me. She had a slightly off-key way of saying things like '*Mais* – you've lost weight!' or '*Tiens!* You're nice and brown!' implying that it was but a matter of days since she had observed you passing her shop looking fat and pasty.

Gigi had arrived in the village in the autumn of 1981. She drove down the Route Nationale 7 from Paris in a van. She rented a shop on the main boulevard, ordered clothes at the *prêt-à-porter* shows and business began.

She sent the women of the village out into the streets to march for the great French art of seduction. She taught them to walk and to sway and to sit, to use cloth as it hadn't been used since the days of Greek and Roman tunics, to fold it in sinuous lapping curves about their bodies, and to tell dramatic stories in cut and colour. Following the drab invasions of the Seventies, the beatnik honey-makers, the bearded potters, the aromatic herbalists on wheat-free diets, Gigi did more to promote the cause of seduction in the village by colour and cut than anyone since Matisse himself. Barcelonaises blew in at the weekends, stepping from their husbands' Mercedes into Gigi's shop, their heels so fabulously high and sharp that barely more than a square centimetre of pavement came into contact with the shoe. They flicked quickly through the hanging clothes, as their grandmothers might have picked over fruit on a market stall, flashing contemptuous looks and buying up all the most extravagant colours.

A circle of women meet there every weekday afternoon. They analyse and dream, unpicking and stitching and altering clothes to suit the shape of the client. They talk in hushed voices. Talk is speculative, vicious, sometimes full of love, sometimes scandalous, sometimes sharp as scissors. They are expert lovers. They have grown-up children and private lives. They read *Elle* and the Goncourt prize winners. They use electrical gadgets to eliminate cellulite and body hair. Towards the end of the afternoon, in winter, they turn on the lamps, take out their spectacles and draw the cloth up closer towards their eyes. They bite needles and pins between their brightly painted lips, and the weak pink inside edges and the pale flesh of their gums show as they break off the thread. The wide balletic movements of their arms throw angular shadows on the shop walls. Now and then their eyes flick up, noting the movements of the villagers along the dog-leg boulevard, in the triangle between the pharmacy, the museum and the café. Gigi's assistant, Pia, fetches a tray of tiny white coffee cups from the bar around the corner. Pia is a plump girl with fine ankles and perfect skin, a Jehovah's Witness. She is a good saleswoman because she is fair but not beautiful. Gigi, who has taught her to pluck her eyebrows, is always complaining that she hides her beautiful baby-soft arms.

Gigi's window is a work of art. Through every season her fibre-glass dolls posture in the tiny window space, cavorting and cocking snooks at the Great Dead Male artists in the museum across the way. Gigi shares with Picasso an eccentric approach to feminine beauty. Better a banshee than a blushing bride, she'll say. A florid complexion can be nicely lit from underneath by a pale-green blouse, a cruelly cut neckline can frame a crepuscular décolleté in vicious relief. She is a mistress of ragtimes in primary colours. She crawls around the window space like a reptile in an illuminated tank, her coffee-coloured hands stroking and teasing at the fabric, tweaking roughly at the mannequins' skirts, lingering at the crotch, teasing out pleats, palms sliding up the insides of their thighs to check for labels that might spoil the lie of the cloth. Or you will see her standing in the doorway of her shop, looking up and down the boulevard, waiting for the lorry, folding her arms and shifting her weight over onto one hip, a ghostly seat for a child now grown.

Women come in, sometimes with their grown-up daughters, sometimes to try and find something that will make them look like their grown-up daughters, sometimes just to chat. And if there are no real customers Gigi's friends sometimes try on the stock and twist and scowl in front of the mirrors. I'd pass Gigi's shop on my way to the postbox at seven in the evening, and Luc would be there, sitting the wrong

47

way round on a chair with his hands up on its back, in his jeans and baggy woollen jumper. He'd be leaning forward and laughing and chatting with the women, saying, no, the colour's not right, try the red one, or try it with the leather coat, and they'd sway up and down in front of him, and he'd pretend not to notice the way they thrust their crotches in his face. Gigi loved it when he dropped in. I suppose it added a *frisson*, having a man around, smoking and bringing a touch of testosterone to the air, which usually smelled of ironing, since Pia steam-ironed the clothes once a week by rotation. He'd smoke a cigarette in the doorway before leaving, so I wouldn't object to the perfume on his clothes. Gigi had one of Luc's paintings on the wall, from his 'femme rose' period, the only time in his life he did anything figurative – female portraits, all done in childish pink paint, with breasts drawn like a W, and often with an angry stab of the brush for a tongue. They were a slap in the face to the notion of feminine beauty the shop proposed, but Gigi had the nerve to hang hers on the wall, like the purloined letter in Edgar Allan Poe's story.

It is difficult to write about Gigi. There is so much I know about her; so much, also, I will never know. What kind of bond exists between women who have shared a lover? When Luc met me there was a kind of official handover of power, but it was one of those handovers where the old regime continues to see to the details of administration in the early days of the new one. She corrected my French. She told me that if I was going to go running I should avoid the boulevard; it wasn't dignified. She would call me in off the street, with her cashmere cardigan draped round her shoulders and a sharpened pencil slid behind her ear.

'Those jeans are hideous,' she would say. 'Where are you going?'

'To the beach.'

'That might pass for chic in London, *chérie*, but here you just look like one more Baba Cool. And after the beach?'

'Dinner at Les Lauriers.'

'What will you wear?'

'The same?'

'No you won't. People will think I've nothing left to sell. Come inside. Take those things off. Put this on. Now.'

She gave me all my best clothes. She gave me her best lover. And sometimes, when we were watching the dancing in the square, or he was standing behind me at a bar, Luc would run his hands over the red dress, the one that clung to my skin as though I had grown inside it from a small seed.

'*Tiens*,' he'd say quietly, so close his lips brushed against my face and I smelled his tobacco, but couldn't see his eyes. 'These are Gigi's hips!'

Refreshments

There are three main cafés on the boulevard. Everyone appears to drink slowly and talk quietly, or maybe it just seems that way because it's out of doors. There is also a *salon de thé* in the square with the fountain. The couple who run it often forget it's their café and that they are the staff. They'll look up from where they are sitting under a parasol, playing cards, with a pot of Darjeeling and a cake each, wondering what's happened to the service.

Angélique's bar is next to the museum. Angélique's brother is a doctor. When I went to him with stomach-ache he gave me a piece of paper which, when I handed it in at the chemist's, turned out to be a prescription for a book – *The Prophet* by Kahlil Gibran. They always have an improving proverb or quotation of the day written up in chalk on the board, and the doctor is their literary adviser. It's not that difficult to come up with something to send the villagers on their way spiritually refreshed: 'An apple a day keeps the doctor away' would sound profound in French. When Angélique changed the name of her bar from Chez Angélique to Papillon Vert for no obvious reason, Luc boycotted it for a few weeks, objecting that any shop, bar or gallery whose title didn't tell you either the name of the owner, or what it sold – and it seemed unlikely Angélique would be serving green-butterfly sandwiches – was inherently suspect. On the whole the French are strikingly straightforward, by English standards, when it comes to naming things. All animals born in one twelve-month period have to be given a name beginning with that year's letter, like a car registration. All streets have abstract tags like Freedom, Republic, Commerce. Even people all seem to share a very small common pool of names. In this way French language resists the Lycra stretch of trans-atlantic English. Stefan, who called his daughter Héloïse, says they keep their fantasy for better things. Angélique and her partner left the village in 1968, when they were eighteen, to hitch-hike to Katmandu, but they only got as far – Luc says, sweetly – as Narbonne.

The three main cafés are the Café de France, the Café du Sport and the Café Central.

A socialist co-operative was set up in 1938 to finance and manage the Café de France – the one with the green umbrellas under the plane trees. Many families still have shares today. They hold their annual general meeting on 2 November, the day of the dead, when the streets are lined with tubs of golden crysanthemums and fallen leaves. After visiting the graves of the dead they convene at the café to go over the accounts. The woman who runs the bookshop opposite decided to start a Café Philosophe in the room upstairs. The first talk of the series was given by a woman who worked in advertising in Perpignan. It was about advertising tech-niques, with a bit of Marcuse thrown in to blot up the many references to her own rapidly expanding busi-ness (cards on the table at the back). Since everything is subject to philosophical consideration in France, she could equally have talked about getting jam to set, or some Himalayan trails. The Café Philosophe becomes the secular equivalent of the Sunday sermon, full of reminders that 'life's a bit like that'.

Two young brothers run the Café du Sport with military efficiency, and polish their photos of Picasso every morning. It's easy to identify the political right, Stefan says, they carry with them an odour of Mr Kleen. They hose the pavement down every night and their chairs are always first out in the morning. It's a good place to drink coffee when it opens at seven thirty, and to read newspapers from Madame Arnoux's next door. In summer the heat crinkles your newspaper by nine, but inside it is chilly and Vanessa Paradis is always on MTV.

On Saturday mornings and summer evenings, clusters of acquaintances, tourists and locals arrange themselves outside the Café Central, opposite the Roman arch, creating patches of alliances, as on a schoolroom map. Ice creams in colours of flesh-pink, pale brown and green sprout like flowers on ornamental shrubs, frothy and crude, and the waiters move in formation between tables with trays on their fingertips, each aware of the others' position, so that if one threw his tray to his colleague at any moment, he could catch it with his spare hand and pass it through his legs to his colleague behind. In summer there are as many English voices as French.

I'd never noticed before how loud an English voice is. I suppose it's less noticeable at home, but here it squawks jaggedly, like a badly played clarinet against a string ensemble. 'Gary, look at this, let's get this for the table; it's cotton, no it's not. Well anyway, it'll wipe, let's get some. Where's Alison gone? Gary! Where's Alison? You take the bags back to the car. No, you, I'm going to find Alison. Where's she gone?'

Of the fifteen restaurants, Les Lauriers and Le Jardin Fleuri have two Michelin stars. Les Lauriers is a graceful building with dark-pink walls and turquoise woodwork, a garden and a slender conservatory which is heated all the year round. The owner is the only female *sommelier* in France. People mostly go for the cheese and the wine, all of them local, all from sources known only to the *sommelière* herself. You peer at the label on the bottle, scribble it down on your napkin, set off to find it the next day, and never do. The same with the cheeses. It's a mystery to me. Les Lauriers votes to the left.

Le Jardin Fleuri is on the road that leads out of the back of the village and up the mountain to the border with Spain – a ten-minute walk from the village. It looks like any glossy hotel with fake-hacienda appeal in any country in the world. It votes to the right.

The pizzeria on the square serves Catalan specialities, *ensalivada*, *boules de picolat*, *pollastre amb gambes*, *la sardinade*, *morue*, *fraginat de Baixas*, and belongs to one of the town's most colourful families, a pair of brothers, perfect examples of the Catalan style, blown up to super-league proportions, so that they are tall, as well as dark-eyed and brown-skinned. I watch their hands and wonder what evolutionary purpose such huge but fine-fingered hands could serve – ropemaking, or calf-delivering, maybe, something for which both size and delicacy would be an asset. Paulo, the younger brother, will often sit out in the afternoon in his suit and a hat on the café terrace, maybe waiting for someone to pass with whom he wants a quiet but public word, which will be delivered painfully, with a stammer – a beguiling impediment in a man of such athletic grace. Janine, his girlfriend, had two boyfriends before him; one of them lisped and the other couldn't pronounce his 'r's. Paulo has huge feet. His drunkenness always seems like a courtesy, to make everyone else feel more relaxed. If drunk enough, he dances, watching his feet come miraculously to life, bending down to gaze at them in astonishment. His brother, Jean-François, runs the bullfighting association and owns a nightclub. They have lived with all the most beautiful women in town, and their present girlfriends look sour and triumphant, knowing they have caught them at the right time, when they are growing tired and want less trouble in their lives.

Activities

There is a list of activities for visitors at the Syndicat d'Initiative – riding, canoeing, thermal baths, Cathar castles – but there are some things it doesn't mention, like swimming at La Cascade, a waterfall concealed in a crack in the hills. There is swimming, too, at La Veyroux – turn right at the sign for the organic duck farm and climb, by car, for another ten minutes or so. Here, the only person you ever meet will be Stefan, reading *Libération* at three in the afternoon in a shady pool, with tiddlers flicking round his thighs. Or you could spend a night wallowing in one of the sulphurous hot pools in the foothills behind the town. You could hire horses and ride up through the mimosa groves and cherry orchards onto the windy hill called le Ventous, from where you can see the sea.

The Museum of Modern Art is open all year round. The inner courtyards are planted with olives, where you can sit out in the sun and peer into the cool white chambers where the paintings are displayed. There's a series of sketches by Matisse, works by Picasso, Derain and the other Fauves, a huge Tàpies, and a collection of local contemporary painters. Opposition to the museum comes from the local painting club, who work up neat miniatures of a cherry orchard with the Canigou in the background and rage at the daubs in the museum by people like Luc, who can't even decide which hand to hold a paintbrush in. At the front entrance a graffiti-style mural by Tàpies confuses foreigners who have boldly asked for directions to the public lavatories and not really unscrambled the reply.

The Cinema shows one film every week, once on a Wednesday for members of the cinema club, and once on a Saturday for the general public. For half an hour at the start of the cinema club someone gives a paper on the film shown the previous Wednesday. Once I heard a lecture on signals of thrust and retreat in *The Bridges of Madison County*, culminating in a frame-by-frame analysis of the scene where Clint Eastwood stops at the traffic lights in the rain. There are sometimes performances at the Salle de Spectacle by Marie-Lou's dance troop – Pierrot and Columbine, Coppélia, Scheherezade. A touring theatre group stops off for a couple of nights four or five times a year and stages a production of something classic with a twist, *Don Quixote*, or *Le Cid*.

But it is a place for being, not for doing. The lie of the land came first, and the people take its shade, respect the way the river runs, the slopes offered to the sun, the blessing of the mountain. *Il faut faire avec*. If you grow up in England you become used to a things-to-make-and-do-on-rainy-days way of looking at the world, learning to adapt it for your pleasure. Of course there are rainy days here, far more than the twenty days a year they will admit to, but for the most part you just watch. You feel the sun on your skin. You do the things God meant you to do. There are only enough hours in a life to do the things you have to do. It is as though God wrote out lots of instructions at the beginning of the world, like 'build cities', 'make maps', 'invent printing press', 'cure the sick', 'discover penicillin' – endless forfeits to be performed the world over, for ever. The instructions round here simply said things like 'walk', 'play with children', 'plant orchard'. Luc had taken the one that said 'sit under tree and watch spider'.

Up at the farm, while a painting dried, he'd sit out under a lime tree with the dog. I'd see him through the window from the sink in the kitchen. I couldn't believe he could spend so long just staring up into a tree. One day, it must have been a Thursday – he didn't work on Thursdays, when he often cut his own hair with a blunt pair of scissors, ending up looking for the next couple of days like a schoolboy with lice who had suffered at the hands of a rough matron – I came out to see if the elderflower had set. Both my former mothers-in-law had tried to teach me how to make elderflower champagne – not that I had been married twice, but my former husband's parents each had, so I'd had two mothers-in-law, each with her own recipe for elder-flower champagne, one much sweeter than the other.

Luc's dog looked up at me, then turned back and stared up at the tree as well. Luc held up his hand and said, very softly, stop. I sat down on the grass beside him. The sleeve of his jumper was daubed with acrylic paint and there were a few stiff grey hairs caught in the wool from that morning's mangled hair-cut. The dog's nose was split, a constant glistening wound, red and wet. She looked round at us, then back up into the tree again. It turned out they had been look-ing not at the tree, or the leaves of the tree, but at a spider, who was abseiling down from a leaf on a rope of spittle, but they could equally well have been watching the tree. He was someone who could watch a leaf for hours. As his focus narrowed – intensified, he said – he would come to concentrate maybe on just one tiny pore, its greenness, its roundness, the leak of moisture, the bite of the leaf's edge. And you, he said to me, you cannot watch a leaf for five seconds without wondering about the breeze that came on the storm that arose from the cloud that was moved by the tug of a gale that came from the switch of a reed of corn in a field where a butterfly's wing moved. He'd go and paint in the early evening, while across the valley someone scythed, or mowed a field with a giant pair of electric shears that swung from a waist harness. In his painting you might see the edge of the leaf, or the pore, drawn with the blunt edge of a stick on the huge paper sheets he stuck together with glue and taped to the floor of the barn. The dog would sit with her front paws crossed over, watching him. She was so happy, loving him, I wished she loved me, too.

2. First Impressions

Leaving home

I was eighteen when I first saw the Canigou, without knowing its name. It was the shape of a clean cutting kitchen instrument against the Mediterranean sky. We'd stopped at the *péage* and were about to cross over into Spain. It was almost the first day of my adult life. I asked the name of the mountain, but I didn't remember it, didn't write it down. Sometimes you ask the name of a thing, of a person, not to remember the name, but the better to remember its face.

I only realized years later that I had come to live in the place I had never forgotten. I was carrying shopping out from one of the huge hypermarkets on the edge of the city by the coast, with the wind turning the stiff palm trees into vicious whips, flaying the air, which was tight and warm as a drum. I looked west towards the mountain, towards the village at the bottom of the valley and thought, Oh, it's here. I came here after all.

I came here without knowing where I was coming to, except that it was the furthest point south you could go in France. I was married to an Englishman. We chose France because it was cheaper than England and we were free to move anywhere in the world. It was the end of the Eighties, we were in our mid-twenties and he was rich.

We bought a huge, ugly house in the bottommost valley of France. It looked like something that might have been built in Cornwall by a tin merchant. It had once been a water mill, and the river flowed through the back garden, no longer wearing away at the walls, but at 300 metres' distance. The parched river bed between the house and the water was a reminder of lost intimacy, of something shrivelled and baked. Now it's overgrown with purple trumpeted buddleia, which attracts orange and white butterflies, and sometimes a grey and black one called Old Lady, as big as my hand. The façade of the house had been remodelled in the nineteenth century, so from the road it looked Gothic and Walt Disney-ish, like somewhere Scooby Doo would have refused to enter.

I moved out one day in August, after three years. I had started telling myself after only a couple of months that 'happiness is not the only way to be happy', in Alice Walker's words. It wasn't surprising it hadn't worked out. Still, I had believed I would stay married to the same man all my life, that from now on there would only be changes here, modifications there, surprises and afflictions, but always the same path; I hadn't thought there would be a moment when I would lose everything – my confidence that I would one day be a mother; the knowledge that when I woke up each morning my garden would be there, and would have grown; the familiar topography of the house; the status of being a wife and having somewhere to welcome people into, someone to lie down next to at night. It was obvious, though, that these were not reasons for staying. I moved out to the town ten kilometres down the road, into a flat opposite the Museum of Modern Art which cost thirty pounds a week to rent. It was three and a half years before I bought the village house.

Suddenly, stripped of everything that had seemed

essential for happiness – a husband, the river running through the garden, the music room with two pianos, my garden, the stream of visitors – I was reminded of happiness itself. I was nearer the Mediterranean than the mountains, and the atmosphere here was more open and relaxed. All I had was this tiny flat; a computer my ex-husband had acquired from his former employers; a wall full of books; a finished, unpublished novel and two small cats. I had a photo album full of wedding shots featuring an alarmed-looking woman and a man looking the way men do when they have spent the afternoon with people shaking their hand and saying, 'Well done!'

Banned, now, from the kind of interminable drink-sodden dinner parties at which ex-pats, in their monstrous stone houses, exercise their spite, snobbery and recipe fetishes; freed from the requirement ever again to comment on the relative advantages of plastic liners over cement-and-tile swimming pools, I found myself looking back at the world I'd been part of with regret only for time misspent. It didn't seem a good idea to stay too high up the valley, being single and female. I carried with me a whiff of adultery most people prefer to keep safely between the covers of their favourite, much-thumbed novels. One woman spat at me in a bar. I didn't realize she was spitting at me; I thought she was consumptive at first, an illness from another age. It turned out it was just a contemptuous gesture from another age. The French, on the other hand, found the public spurning of me and the abusive phone calls hilarious, like a Beaumarchais play. It heightened the atmosphere in the little flat, which overlooked the church roof and set me nose to nose with the pigeons.

There were awful lonely days at the beginning. I'd fall asleep in the early afternoon. Sleep seemed the only way of reconnecting with what was familiar. I'd fall so deep into the well my head would implode and I'd wake up still inside my sleep, paralysed, shouting out but making no noise. I read somewhere that this was quite common and was to do with momentary paralysis of the brain. When I eventually managed to wake myself I'd walk about the flat, banging into the walls, unable to judge the width of doorways, the spaces between the chairs, like being reborn fully adult, but ignorant of how to feed, walk or phone the emergency services.

I hardly knew anyone in the town. We'd lived for three years up the valley, and only occasionally came this far down for the market, or sometimes to eat. I knew a few French people, but not the ones I wanted to know. I didn't want to go home. I wanted to be part of the landscape, to have a right to live in it, to drop my accent, speak southern French, and have all the time in the world you need for those extra syllables Parisians never use. Stepping out of the ex-pat world was like stepping out of an isolation tent into contact with the smell, touch and weight of things.

My first real friend was Duncan, who stood up for the scarlet woman in me because he'd always fancied being one himself. He also dreamed of being a lady novelist. When I stopped at the postbox of my old house one day and found a month-old letter from a publisher offering me a contract, he said I was fulfilling his life's ambitions by becoming both at once.

Duncan kept goats and made cheese and had moved to the valley from Leicester in the Seventies. He had four children and the younger three had stayed there with their mother, living in a feminist commune. The eldest, Ben, was now at university. He had run away to join his father when he was seven, and then he'd run away from his father and the milk churns when he was fourteen on his horse. Arriving at Luc's farm, he asked for a glass of water and stayed for three years. Ben never went to school, but his father had a huge library, and so he was immensely well read. When he got to university he discovered that he had read everything on the reading list for the three-year course by the time he was twelve, but he didn't know the order of the letters of the alphabet, or the months of the year. Even now, if you ask him the months of the year he can't recite them, he has to work them out.

Duncan looked after me with disinterested kindness and passion, not for me, but for the act of looking after me. He had a succession of beautiful, malicious girl-friends, who bullied him, stamped on his glasses in the middle of the road, slept with his friends, seduced his son and threw paint at his walls. He was utterly poverty-stricken, camp and butch; the funniest, most petulant, most selfish, extravagant man I'd ever met; gay as a daisy one minute, macho the next. To me he was only ever kind. He spent hours sawing wood by hand during the day and mending fences. At night he made little dishes of goat's liver.

He read me the short stories of Gabriel García Marquez, *Giles Goat Boy* by John Barth, Patricia Highsmith, Georges Simenon, *The Persian Boy* by Mary Renault, something different every night. He called me the synchronicity kid, because, he said, wherever I went coincidences came hurtling out of the sky. He could walk to his bookshelf, where there were over 2,000 volumes, pick up any book and open it at the page with my name on it. Either that or 'goat'. His cry, one evening, when he opened a book by Marquez and fell on the first page of a story about a goat with the same name as me sent my cats skittering from the fire and out into the night. One of them, a ginger kitten, was eaten by a fox.

Duncan had told me about Luc. He was born here. Not only is he the village dentist, he said, he is also an artist, and he paints *horrible* pictures, and sells them in Paris, and he is *terribly* clever and bitter and my son loves him. He sounded right up my street. Strangely, because Duncan was always pushing me towards men, but then maybe only the men he fancied himself, he never imagined me with Luc. Luc himself says he first saw me one Saturday morning in the café, talking to Duncan and laughing. Luc found Duncan tedious because he laughed too much, too loud, but since I seemed, in public at least, quite well behaved, he told Ben to introduce us.

Meeting Luc

The day Ben and I first drove up to the farm it was already growing dark. It was a Sunday in February. We were in my Renault 5. The road out of the town led south. Ahead you saw a bank of high hills, the same ones you can see from the house in the village. The road bends left and right, zigzagging upwards towards the border. It was to become such a familiar journey. Now I can't recall if the dog at the geranium house on the ninth corner barked that day as it did on all the days of the years that came after, or if I was aware of the grey Mediterranean in the gulf behind us, a Sunday afternoon sea in winter, strung with faint white lights along the coast, and the railway track running along beside it.

We turned in at a green gate. It was like lurching from Pagnol to Proust, from something dry and brittle, taut with winter resin, to an elegant avenue of limes and rhododendron, with a summer house here, and on the left an overgrown tennis court. Then the avenue became a track and the world turned Mediterranean again, with two squat farmhouses and two black horses sleeping standing up. Across the fields was a line of trees. They looked as though they had been torched, but in fact they were just about to come into leaf. There was a moribund feel to the place. It was somewhere of which people would say, 'It's so beautiful,' but you could tell they were glad they didn't live there themselves.

He was standing by the door, outside, fetching wood from the pile at the front of the house. I didn't see him till we were close up to the door, and then he appeared out of the dark. His ex-wife used to say he could levitate sideways, so you could be quite sure he was next door, asleep, or reading, and then you'd feel his breath on your face. He smiled at me, and I felt like a plant set back in softly forked earth, packed gently into place. The world had become familiar again, possible again, because he was in it, though I had never seen him before. When Ben introduced me he said, 'I know.'

Luc lived alone. His life was austere, his living space completely spartan. Any one of the rooms in his house could have been the tack room – saddles and bridles hung from trestles, oilskin coats and hats from hooks screwed into the walls. It was everyone's idea of the perfect, remote French farmhouse. It was desperately uncomfortable, had two barns, which he used for painting, and a rat lived in the bathroom. I was always poised to leap onto a chair. Sometimes, when there was a silence between us and I was lying on the grass with my head on his stomach looking up at the leaves, he would wait till my breathing was deep and relaxed and then would say, 'Do you know how they discovered I had tapeworm?' I'd yell, 'Stop!' and leap away from him and run. Once I jumped onto his horse without stirrups or a saddle, an unprecedented act of athleticism, and kicked her to a gallop from standing still. When I came back he was waiting on the step outside the tack room. He said severely, 'You should never make her gallop from cold like that. It's bad for her.'

When I apologized he said quietly, 'That's all right. By the way, did I ever tell you . . . ?'

We sat by the fire and drank a kind of white pastis from an old monastery Luc often rode to on a Sunday. The fire was hot and spat out gobbets of flame. 'Do you have children?' he asked. 'No,' I said, 'not yet. And you?' 'No,' he said, 'not yet.' He took us to see his paintings.

'The museum are making *postcards* of them for the exhibition,' he said. '*Quelle époque!*' He painted on huge stretches of brown wrapping paper, stuck several times to itself, with acrylic paints. At first I was horrified by what he painted. I couldn't see it at all. I didn't understand what he was doing. Later I wrote two books in his house. He was always asking me to translate a page or two for him, but I never did. It made him angry, and he'd say, 'It's as though you couldn't actually *see* my paintings, but you do, you see them all the time.' I wasn't sure I did really see them. He'd show me a new one and say, '*Tu le vois?*'

'What's for supper?' Ben asked.

'*Confit de canard.*' I was impressed. Months afterwards I asked if they'd really had *confit de canard* that night, because we certainly hadn't since.

'Why not?' Luc said. 'Even I can open a tin.'

'Stay for supper,' he said. 'Ben's staying, then I'm driving him back to college.'

'I'm not hungry. We had a late lunch.'

'*L'appétit vient en mangeant.*' The more you have the more you want.

I had to leave anyway because I was meeting someone in the café later on. We had to sit on the edge of a table because they'd cleared away all the chairs, for some reason. Outside they were burning life-sized papier-mâché dolls; it was the last day of the carnival. At one point in the evening Luc walked into the café and bought a packet of cigarettes. I thought it must be his brother because I'd never seen him before that afternoon, and it seemed too much of a coincidence to bump into him again already. It was him, though. Like me, he had a way of looking different every time you saw him. People were never sure, when they saw us together, that it was really us.

People don't walk into your life. They were there all along, but you couldn't see them. That day, he emerged from invisibility. He told me that he was someone who, if you didn't know him, was invisible. 'Wait and see,' he said. 'Now you know who I am you'll see me all the time.'

First day

The next morning I went out to buy bread. The baker I normally went to was shut on Mondays, so I went to a new one. While I was waiting in the queue, Luc walked in, whistling. He had a breathy whistle, like a leaking pipe. The baker's wife came out from behind the counter, kissed him and gave him a pot of quince jelly. '*Pour ta maman.*'

'*Salut,*' he said, as though we met there every morning.

I said, 'Aren't you going to work today?'

He was wearing the same clothes he'd been wearing the previous evening. He frowned. 'Of course I am. I'm not a tourist.'

When we came out, me with my baguette in a wisp of paper and him with his croissant and his pot of quince, he said '*Tiens*, I've got something to show you.' We walked back up to the boulevard. It was so hot that the newsagents had all put out their postcard stands for the first time that year, and the sandwich shop next to the museum had set up its yellow umbrellas. Luc looked at them and said softly, '*Quelle idée!*'

It was like the rising credits of a film. In fifty yards of street on a Monday morning we met all the people who would feature in our life. We bumped into Marie-Lou, yawning on her way to give a dance class, and passed the chemist, opening up his shop window, where he displayed miniature replicas of prosthetic equipment you could order from him – tiny wheelchairs and miniature toilets for the disabled, and next to them a chart showing which local mushrooms were safe to pick and which to leave, and a couple of taxidermied poisonous snakes. Luc waved at Gigi, who was crawling around inside her shop window, fixing pleats on a mannequin. Stefan slipped out of a doorway with *Libération* under his arm. The doctor was writing up a motto on a blackboard outside his sister's coffee shop. That morning it said, '*La dernière chose qu'on trouve en faisant un ouvrage est de savoir celle qu'il faut mettre en premier*' – the last thing you realize on constructing a work is what to put first. '*C'est Pascal*,' Luc said. '*Quel con.*'

We stopped outside the Museum of Modern Art, opposite my rented apartment. Luc said, 'Meet me here at midday. I'm hanging my pictures for Friday.' He pointed upwards. 'That's what I wanted to show you.'

'The sky?'

'No, that.'

There was a huge banner draped from a pole over the façade of the building with his name on it. 'Don't forget,' he said and went off to open his surgery. I waited till he'd gone round the corner, then bought a postcard.

At midday I found him standing next to the spinner outside the newsagent, talking to a man with paralysed hands. He introduced us and I held out my hand, but the man didn't respond. Luc took my hand instead, and led me into the museum. Inside it was so pale and cool I got goose pimples. A woman with silky brown hair came rushing down the stairs with her cardigan round her shoulders, like a Fifties heroine, scolding him from a distance. Luc dropped my hand and shrugged, with a smile.

'I've been waiting for you all morning,' she cried angrily. 'Where've you been?'

'Here she is,' he said proudly, as though he'd just made me. 'She's English.'

I was wearing a green cotton dress with red flowers on it from Monsoon. She looked at me coldly and said, 'Yes, I can see that.'

We went into the main gallery. Luc's paintings were already up. I'd seen them flat on the floor of the barn the evening before, and now they looked as if they'd staggered to their feet for an inspection, and were momentarily slumped back against the walls because they had a hangover or were desperate for shade. The shoddy, temporary look was accentuated by the fact that they were a bit off-centre, and stuck to the wall with drawing pins – Luc's choice. One was a deep, thick marine blue, with a bone-white loop and a bit at the bottom that looked as though he'd kicked a bucket of paint over when standing back to judge the effect. I caught myself thinking like my mother. I screwed up my eyes. That was better; it looked like a painting again.

I looked around the different rooms, read some letters in a case, written by Picasso to his first wife, Fernande Olivier. Luc and the woman, who turned out to be the curator of the museum, came up the stairs. She was still scolding him fondly in a way that made it obvious they had once been lovers. I wondered whether, if he and I ever became lovers, we would fall out and I would talk to him in that way. It seemed unlikely, but he did have that effect on people. Even men talked to him like that, I noticed. He was laughing and saying, '*Mais non, mais non!*' He almost never raised his voice, as though there was a part of himself he particularly didn't want to disturb.

He found me looking at a series of lithographs by

Matisse. '*Tu aimes ça?*' he asked. I was pretty sure I liked Matisse, but how could you actually tell? You looked, and you thought, That's definitely Matisse, and because you were so pleased to recognize someone you knew, you didn't actually care too much whether you liked them or not. The museum also had a series of late Picasso drawings on the theme of the artist, the monkey and the model. Luc pointed out how rapid the strokes were, how hasty the execution; it had never occurred to me before to think about the speed of a work of art.

'Come and look at this,' he said, putting his arm round my shoulder. I was reminded of the donkey boy who had found me, lost, on the beach at Scarborough when I was two or three. He had taken me to a hut, where we had stayed for what seemed like days. Luc was looking after me. He was enacting the gestures of love.

You can't love someone from the start. It is something you realize has happened, like a payment made into a bank account while you weren't looking. Until that time, lovers act out the emotion and make shapes which love, later on, will inhabit. The French call it '*Jouer la comédie de l'amour*'.

Up another flight of stairs, he led me to a painting signed with his name. It was a huge matt-black rectangle, with a white scribble, and in the middle a pair of photocopied eyes.

'Is that—?' It looked like his work, a bit, but like what you might expect him to be doing in fifty years' time. I was glad I hadn't said so, though, because it turned out it was by his uncle.

'That's my grandmother,' he said. 'Those are her eyes. He took it with a Kodak before they carried her off to the mortuary.' As a First World War widow – her husband's name was on the base of the Maillol

74

memorial, killed early on in the war, in 1914 – she had had special privileges, in particular a licence to open a post office in the big house on the boulevard. Luc owned it now, though his parents and uncle lived there.

The uncle painted on meticulously prepared black canvases, thick-coated with a special matt-black paint he got sent up from Barcelona. He'd Scotch tape the eyes to the canvas and scribble something in chalk underneath. That was the only kind of picture he ever did now.

'She was a fossil anyway,' Luc said, 'long before she died. She'd sit at the drawing-room window, up on the second floor, looking out on the street with the phone book on her lap. Whenever anyone passed by she'd call out their telephone number off the top of her head, then she'd check it against their entry in the book.'

Outside, on the terrace, he pointed out the roof of my flat. 'You could sunbathe on it.' I did, later that afternoon, even though it was only February. The tiles were hot and dangerous, and if I'd fallen asleep I would have ended up rolling off into the street. 'Come to the opening on Friday night,' he said. 'And to dinner afterwards in the square.'

That evening, and every evening that week, I saw him walking the boulevard with his uncle, a shrunken brown man with a nose like the child catcher's in *Chitty Chitty Bang Bang*. He wore a sky-blue jumper, a colour from a crayon box. Luc would lift his hand, smile and carry on.

The second evening I saw him outside the café. He was wearing a startling green jumper, the synthetic apple green of children's sweets. He had one leg up on one of the municipal flower pots, and I could see a stretch of skin between his shoe and where his jeans began. It was the winter brown of someone who is tanned all year round. I thought it was because it was Luc that I'd started noticing things like that, but I think actually it was because I'd just turned thirty. He nodded to me and said, '*Hep!*' a greeting he normally used for horses. The woman he was talking to was Vietnamese and was crying. He was talking very quietly. He had the strongest accent du midi I'd ever heard. Sometimes I thought he was joking, his e's at the end of words were so heavy it sounded like a bad rhyme in a litany or a hymn, and his voice was both deep and very soft, with, just occasionally, a metallic tang.

Suddenly it seemed like he was king of the village. I saw him walking with everyone, leaning against every wall and laughing, coming out of every shop, drinking in every café. It reminded me of my old comics, when you had to find hidden objects in the picture on the front cover – twenty squirrels, four buckets, two lawn mowers. There were at least twenty Lucs hidden in the village at any given minute of the day, and I only had to walk round a corner to bump into one of them.

Opening

The Museum of Modern Art had once been the police station. It had been turned into the museum in the 1950s. Picasso gave them a series of fifty-six ceramic bowls, painted with moments from a bullfight, as a start-up pack. Reconditioned at the end of the Eighties, the building now looked as though it had been given a makeover to keep up with the times and the company it kept. Since it had reopened one night in June 1993 there had been two big shows, one of Miró graphics and the other Tàpies, from Barcelona. Luc was the first local painter to exhibit. He was also one of a number of local painters who sold their work in Paris. His *galeriste* – gallery owner – was a tall, stooped Belgian of seventy-five, who lived in the Place des Vosges. The gallery was on the Rue de Seine and had black walls. They did a lot of body art there in the Seventies – people burning their bodies with candles and making incisions in their flesh. Now he stopped at Notre Dame every morning and lit a candle for his young painters. Luc felt this was a bit too much of a spiritual approach to hustling, but since he had an ambivalent attitude to success, and would always say, '*Quelle calamité,*' if he heard of someone selling a painting for a large sum of money, he couldn't really complain.

Passing the café shortly after two o'clock on the day

of the opening, I was trying to fit new batteries into my Walkman. Luc waved and called me over. He was sitting with about six other men, none of them local, all drinking *citron pressé*. He introduced me. They were all painters or gallery owners. Everyone kept moving around to keep the elderly Belgian dealer in the shade. Luc fixed up my Walkman and said in a low voice, without looking at me, 'Your shoes are *très jolies*,' and I thought, An Englishman would never say that.

I was surprised to find him with these people, and that they were his friends. Until then I had only seen him in the streets of the village or on the farm. I realized later that the farm was the polar opposite, in its male austerity, to his parents' cut-glass world, where things could so easily be broken. As I left he caught my shoulder and said, very quietly, 'In future, don't wear a Walkman in the street, *coquine*. It makes you look like a tourist.'

In the evening I got to the opening late, having been caught up in a conversation with my ex-husband – maybe it was the day he came round and fetched the furniture away. A dignified gentleman from Gloucestershire who lived up the valley had also rung me and said, 'You're a liar and a cheat and my wife never wishes to speak to you again.' I imagined him rehearsing the words before he picked up the phone, masticating them stickily, like a preacher in a bathroom mirror. I was not in the mood for seduction. Did I really want this with Luc? Maybe my taste in men was a bit strange. They had to have something of the sea about them, to be deep, quiet and mysterious, but with playful currents and as many moods. It never occurred to me that you could be happy with someone you didn't need to watch night and day just to stop yourself drowning.

At the opening the mayor was wearing his green silk

suit and making a speech. Luc was smiling warily. Everybody wanted a bit of him. I wasn't sure I did yet, so I waved at him, looked at his pictures and quickly left, along with a woman wrapped in a thick sheepskin coat who was sneezing and trembling. She introduced herself as his ex-wife.

'He warned me not to come,' she said. 'He *told* me.'

Later I learned he'd also telephoned his best friend, a psychoanalyst in Paris, and told him, 'Don't come. Just don't come. I don't want you here.' The friend came anyway, took a room at the hotel and went to look at the pictures the following morning.

I said, 'Why did he say that? And why did you come? Weren't you angry with him?' Marcel said no, he wasn't angry, you had to give and take with Luc. Give what? Take what? I wondered.

I didn't go to the dinner, but at eleven o'clock someone called for Ben and asked me to give him a message. I went round to the restaurant. About thirty people were sitting at an L-shaped table. I gave Ben the message; '*Il te cherchait*,' he said. I hadn't noticed Luc, but at that moment I felt his hand fall on my shoulder.

'I'm sorry,' I said, turning. 'I didn't come.'

'We're just going outside,' he told the others. 'Back soon.'

The streets were empty. There was a strong moon and a hectic sky of racing clouds. '*Allez*. Lezz-go,' he said. It was his one phrase of English. I thought he'd said, 'Let go,' and dropped his arm. 'It will be windy up the mountain,' he said. 'Take my coat.'

He never made me any proposition. He never told me he was in love with me or that he desired me. 'He kept saying, "She's so sweet, so *gentle*",' Stefan said later. 'He never said you were beautiful at all.' He showed me his house, his horses, his paintings. He said, this is it, this is my life. He opened his entire world to me. He never asked me to accept him. It was as though everything had happened before we met, or in the moment we met. It was my first ever relationship without language, without promises or assurances or confirmations of any kind.

3. Useful Background

The History of the Mas

The estate had not been in his family for long. It had once belonged to a *pied noir* bishop with a diocese in North Africa, who'd had it built at the turn of the century. The bishop had had no – recognized – offspring, so eventually it passed to a distant relative, Monsieur Desarthes, a surgeon at the hospital in Toulouse. Monsieur Desarthes was drafted during the Second World War, and later found himself, in the company of Luc's father, in a prisoner-of-war camp on the French–German border. They became friends, and when Monsieur Desarthes retired from the hospital he spent his summers on the estate for the good of his health. He suffered from rheumatoid arthritis, and Luc's father, as the village doctor, treated him, mostly with good conversation and whisky, until he died.

One day his widow called at the house after surgery hours. Sitting perched on the edge of the chaise longue, like a bird on its cage trapeze, she said that she had come to discuss the division of her estate. She and her husband had agreed, before he died, that the estate should be given to the doctor's family, since they had none of their own.

There were three properties on the estate. Two of them were farmhouses, facing each other on the inner thighs of two adjoining mountains. The first was a roofless shell called Mas Breillat, close up by the Spanish border, perhaps two kilometres away as the crow flies, two hours' ride through the forest, crossing the river and climbing again up the opposite slope. It was entirely overgrown now, but featured on maps of the mountain in the seventeenth century, when it might have been the house of a woodcutter or a shepherd. Madame Desarthes gave this one directly to Luc. The second farmhouse was a much larger, colder mas and was named Teissarde, after the bishop. It comprised two separate, solid dwellings. This was given to Luc and his older brother, Georges, to split between them.

Fifty yards away from Mas Teissarde, but separated in time by at least three centuries, was a bourgeois summer house, built by the bishop, with bleached wooden floors and a huge terrace facing west to the Canigou. This would go to the parents, to use as a weekend retreat. I imagined myself in it, wearing a plain white dress with my hair coiled into the nape of my neck, married to a Lutheran pastor whom I was betraying with his young curate. It was what Stefan called the Ingmar Bergman effect, a standard fantasy of European women, daughters of Lutherans and Methodists, who get caught up at the crossroads of passion and guilt, Protestantism and Catholicism, and end up in a Mediterranean world, hiding their necks from the sun.

The two sons were both born in the house which used to be the surgery, so they had both been brought up in the village, and had no experience of the mountains when they were young.

Madame Desarthes handed over the estate some years before she died. She liked to see it lived in and would occasionally visit in the afternoons in early or late summer. In the drawing room of the summer house there was a Steinway, which she played, laying aside her stick and hitching up her long skirts. She had always worn white until the death of her husband. After that she only ever wore black. Luc remembers her standing on the terrace, looking over the valley at the Canigou, wearing a huge, flat black hat and with a narrow, pinched coat on over her dress, a stick and a parasol. It seems rather a lot at once, and I wonder whether he hasn't accumulated a number of different props from different scenes.

At the time of the bequest, Luc had already begun painting his huge abstract pictures inspired by the landscape. He was twenty and studying to be a dentist at the university in Marseilles. He wanted a job that would allow him to work two days a week and spend the rest of the time painting, for the rest of his life, without ever having to cross over the Pont du Diable. Madame Desarthes doted on Luc because he had written to France Musique for her while she had been ill the previous winter and got hold of a ticket to a concert in their studios in Paris the following spring, which gave her something to get better for. He was, as he often pointed out himself, one of those people who make things better. This was quite a strange gift, because he was explosive and could be unkind and maniacal. But if you had a problem of which he wasn't the cause he was a veritable healer. The summer he came of age Luc turned his back on the sea, and went up into the mountains. He took with him the woman who would live with him for the next twelve years. He married her after eleven and a half years, then divorced her six months later. Like him, she had lived in the village all her life, but he first saw her that summer, sitting at a café table, and identified her as someone he could love.

Like Luc, Catherine floated when she walked. She

was thin and brown and serene, and she had a voice that soothed you when your own throat was raw. She played the piano, was a star pupil at the local lycée and had just won a place to study at a lycée in Paris for a year before applying to university. Her father was a colonel. He had married the elder of two sisters, had Catherine, then divorced and married the younger sister, had two boys, then divorced and married the elder one again, so that Catherine's aunt was also her ex-stepmother, and her mother was her half-brothers' stepmother and aunt.

Hearing that she was about to go to Paris to begin her year's study as he was about to go off to a southern university to study medicine, Luc went and fetched his car – the doctor's cast-off – and drove Catherine up the mountain to Mas Breillat. The drive takes about forty minutes. After that you have to walk for half an hour. As they came round the corner, in view of the pile of stones, he watched her face, and when he saw her move towards it as she would later move towards her horses, gently, unafraid, he said he knew she wouldn't go to Paris to the lycée, she'd stay there and fix up the house with him.

The colonel was furious and went marching round to see Luc's parents – his daughter must have an education; she was a brilliant student who could do well for herself. He wasn't going to stand for her shacking up with the doctor's son, fixing up his pile of stones for him while he was off getting his degree in Marseilles. 'And you'd better marry her, too, while you're about it. This is a respectable family you're dealing with here.' 'Oh, really?' Luc replied. Catherine went to Paris, stayed six weeks, cut all her lessons and spent her afternoons sitting in the Jardin des Plantes writing letters to Luc about the city and how she was dying of urban blight, so he went up and fetched her home.

They lived at Mas Breillat for eleven years. Catherine cooked and put the roof on, while Luc worked in the dental surgery down in the village. At first she wrote poetry, but soon became discouraged. Like Luc, she would look out of the window and say, 'The real thing's better.' Eventually they moved to Teissarde, the big farm, and began keeping horses, always Catherine's dream. Georges, who was already living in his half of the big farm, resented Luc's arrival and decided to make a property issue out of it. He said that if he ever found one of Luc's horses or his dog on his bit of land, on the wrong side of the hawthorn hedge, he would shoot them. For the first six months everything went fine. But one of Luc's painter friends kept his horses at the house, too, and one day he brought his wife, Anne, over to ride. Catherine saw the look on Luc's face. He was never clandestine. Deceit would not have suited him at all. The following day, clearing his path, she left.

On their last night together they slept outside, as they had often done since the time they had no roof, under a blanket, with the sound of his horses munching close to their ears as they cropped the grass around their bodies. They'd always huddled up close, as people do when there is no bed. When there is no bed you feel more of an urge to touch the other person. But that last night he slept in the meadow and she slept in front of the house, under the lime tree. At first the dog sat with her, licking her face. But whenever Catherine fell asleep the dog would slope off and lie down beside him. When she heard her mistress stirring she would get up and go over to her again, as though a bell had rung. Eventually Catherine pushed her away, sending her back to Luc. '*Va avec lui. Je pars. Tu restes là*' – I'm leaving. You stay there.

The men in this family are so obsessed with their

past, she said, that suffering in the present leaves them unmoved. They suffer, but do not react. They accept endings without even wincing. When she drove away, Luc stood in the drive, watching her go; but before she had driven out of the gate he had already started talking to his dog, ruffling her ears as they walked back together towards the house.

A week later he heard someone talking on *France Culture* about a man who'd left someone called Catherine for a woman called Anne and he thought, It's me! *C'est mon histoire!* but when he told his friend Henri, the cardiologist, he said no, he'd heard the same programme, and actually they'd been talking about Henry VIII. Now Catherine lives with a carpenter, who has the biggest hands I've ever seen on any man. He learned to read and write in prison before he met her, but Catherine does the books. Luc gave her Mas Breillat, where she grows aromatic flowers and St John's Wort, which is effective for depression. She and Bertrand live off maybe 700 francs a week. She could get a job, teach, give riding lessons, run an art gallery, manage a restaurant, but she would rather be poor. She lives with the love of her life. They have no children; she is her husband's child, and she has accepted that. When the village was alight with celebrations after the bullfight one year, I saw them stroll through the crowd together, he with his huge arm, the size of Luc's thigh, round her shoulder, and she with her dark head against him, both looking as if they were walking on water. Later on they danced as a Spaniard in silk slacks sang 'O mio bambino caro' through speakers as big as the Roman gate. Bertrand's eyes were full of tears. As we leaned against the café wall, Luc followed my eyes and said, 'You see, I did her a favour, leaving her. Thanks to me she's discovered the love of her life.'

Family Affairs

The first morning I spent at the mas was a Sunday, and I slept through the cockerel crowing and woke to a low keening bellow, emitted by a dying cow. Georges's herd grazed just yards away from the bedroom, on the other side of a bank edged with hawthorn. Luc's first thought on hearing the cow's bellow was that Georges would think he had poisoned it, or stabbed it in the gullet with a paintbrush.

He pulled on his outdoor clothes like a child, in two movements, slid his feet into his riding boots and went out onto the terrace and down into the field. The cow was groaning, trying to deliver its dead foetus, which was already poisoning its blood. I got up and looked for the kettle. It's the best thing you can do in a strange house, find the kettle. It always feels like an ally of sorts, as though you'd met before.

In the meadow, Georges was talking with his hands, placing things in the air. Brigitte, his wife, was standing with her arms crossed, staring at the cow. Luc was calmly walking back towards the house with his dog at his heel. I never saw him run. His life was an andante, but understrung with a tight, restraining web of wires; you always felt there was a quicker man straining to be unleashed, if only he'd allow it. He came into the kitchen, picked his hat off the peg by the door and opened the fridge. '*Alors, coquine?*' He smelled of leather and paint. There was coffee in a tin pot over the cooker. From out of the bottom compartment of the fridge he took a small glass jar. In the drawer under the hat peg he found a syringe, tilted it to the light, then drew some liquid out of the glass jar, took the coffee cup from me, drank it down, and went out again carrying the syringe, which he kept for emergencies with the horses, in case he ever had to put one down, if it was hurt or ill. From the terrace, by the winter wisteria, laid out like a ruined fishing net on the wall, I watched as he knelt down by the cow and sank the needle into its side. The dog stepped back and looked away into the distance, where the horses had gathered to drink from a stone trough under a lime tree, mulching leaves into the damp earth and slurping noisily. The aching moan of the cow ceased. Luc removed his hand from her flank and stood up slowly. Then Brigitte fetched the tractor from the barn and they tied the carcass to its rear end and dragged it slowly away.

Luc came back, whistling very softly under his hat. The dog walked like a maid of honour, attentive and proud, just inches behind him. I was doing the washing-up, trying to balance a plate against a pan on the stone draining board.

'Look. All the water just sits there in a puddle.'

'You're right,' he said, considering me. He was pleased I had at least some practical sense. He'd expected none of what he called a city woman. 'I'll make you an *égouttoir* out of sycamore twigs.' It became a private joke. He'd make me a dish drainer one of these days. Every month he claimed the design was almost finished, that he just had to refine it slightly, or that he'd had a better idea and would have to start from scratch all over again. Likewise with the bath, which had no plug. You had to stuff a flannel in the hole and lay a rock on top of it. Luc claimed it worked on suction, that if you laid the flannel correctly it would clamp itself into the hole, but I found it was an egg-timer bath, that you could only stay in six minutes before the water all ran out and your time was up.

Georges and Brigitte had moved onto the farm and bought their first cow while Luc and Catherine were still living on the opposite side of the mountain. Georges was supposed to be studying to become a surgeon, but quietly began breeding a surreptitious dairy herd, until the day came when the doctor and his wife could no longer pretend not to have noticed that their elder son had become a farmer and was never going to finish his education. They blamed the spirit of 1968, which had turned the young people's heads. In the early Seventies, disenchanted students from the north had arrived, with their anti-metropolis, anti-technological ideas, and put their political science degrees to use, producing goat's cheese and honey. Thirty years on they are all leaping onto the Web, so you can get *crottin de chèvre* online, direct from the producer. People like Luc's mother, who wouldn't have dreamed of going for a walk in the countryside without her best boots, an elegant coat and her poodle on a leash, found the cheesecloth and rats' tails approach to country life quite incomprehensible, and considered subsistence farming a scandalous risk to public health.

Over the years tension grew, along with the herd. Georges accused his parents of sabotaging the engine of his car – a serious accusation considering the route down to the village involved fifteen hairpin bends. Then he claimed to have discovered that his parents had arranged to have legal custody over him, for which he needed to be declared insane. Until the week I met them all, he hadn't spoken to his parents for fifteen years. I couldn't understand this, because they seemed nice, the kind of parents you might wish you could trade your own for after an irritable Christmas.

Their mother was a beautiful woman, the only other blonde in the village apart from me, people said knowingly – *Bluff your Way in Freud*. 'I am the happiest mother alive,' she said to me at the supermarket checkout one morning, just after we met, eyeing my two tins of tuna and passing before me with her three kilos of fresh lobster, for which she would produce a perfect *sauce à l'armoricaine* the following Sunday, Easter Sunday, when she had invited the entire family to lunch. Clearing out the cupboard after her death, I found twenty tiny-sized tins of *sauce à l'armoricaine*. She was, in fact, the perfect Fifties housewife. Today the perfect housewife would make her own, and you have to wonder who is the freer of the two.

She was happy because that very week Georges had visited her in their house in the Rue St Florian for the first time in maybe fifteen years, and had sat fidgeting in an armchair for half an hour, telling her that her poodle was badly trained and asking who got the beach house in the will. It was his way of being intimate. I don't think it can have been much fun for Brigitte being alone with him for twenty years on the farm. It emerged that Georges had decided to make peace with his parents, or at least to drop the accusations for a while, because things had started going wrong with Brigitte, his common-law wife. He needed to drum up some family support.

He suffered from advanced marital paranoia, and his reason was severely affected by his conviction. He firmly believed that whenever friends came over to chat in their kitchen about Rudolf Steiner, organic farming and esoteric texts, Brigitte would leave the room not to turn the cheese in the dairy, but to make love to one of those not present, who had prearranged the whole thing with the others behind his back.

At first she laughed at his accusations. Physically she was a strong woman, with tight, curly grey hair, the body of an eighteen-year-old boy and eyes that were the strange milky blue of the veins in a mother's breast. Later she protested her innocence. She had never looked at another man. For twenty years she had only ever looked at the earth, and occasionally at the sky to see if it would rain. He lost his fear of her, fearlessness being one of the side effects of anger and despair. She started to panic. She had no rights; she had no possessions apart from her piano; she had no children. I thought that if she'd ever been able to love him in the first place, then she must still do. But by the time of the Easter Sunday lunch she was in despair.

Easter Sunday

That meal, the first of many, was unlike any event I had ever attended. We arrived from the four corners of the estate, converging on the doorstep of the summer house. Architecturally, it was like going to Argentina for the day. The night before, it had snowed. Marcel, Luc's psychoanalyst friend from Paris, had arrived with his newly born baby grandson. It was 21 March, the first day of spring, the sky was as clean and sharp as a newly beaten sheet of metal. Luc had written '*Coucou!*' in the snow, to greet the baby. As we crossed over to the summer house the next morning, we found crocuses beaded with melted snow in the patchy grass where he'd written hello.

It was a desiccated house. Everything in it, including the lives lived, seemed to belong to an entirely different age. Some skulls and the family teeth were kept in a cupboard in one of the bedrooms, along with the robes of the late bishop. In the cellar hung row upon row of decaying wooden tennis racquets. I liked to picture the bishop frolicking on the tennis lawn in his gold and purple robes and hat, swatting butterflies and buffeting about for his lost ball among the rhododendrons.

In the long drawing room there was a fire burning in the grate. Luc's father clasped me to him tenderly and rasped some inaudible words in my ear while his poodle danced up my skirt, stamping peanuts into the floorboards. Then the doctor went round with the champagne, slender-stemmed glasses trembling on a silver tray. His wife took me by the hand and led me upstairs, past posters for bullfights from the last century, and a photograph of a cousin, an operatic tenor who had moved to Argentina, where he had died on stage during the second act of *Turandot*. We went and inspected the linen cupboard. I had never seen so much pristine cotton, so stiff it would be like sleeping between boards. By the time we came back downstairs again, Georges and Brigitte had arrived. Brigitte grabbed my hand and pulled me out onto the terrace. I was a wild card being passed around the family, with a different value according to what each of them already held in their hand. It was a beautiful day, and the Canigou was still dredged in last night's snow. Her face was almost corrugated with grief. 'She showed you the linen?' she said, gripping my hand. Yes, I said, she had. I hoped she wasn't thinking of work for these apparently idle hands to do. Brigitte let go of my hand. She stepped to the edge of the terrace and rolled a tiny cigarette, striking a match on the wall. She breathed in through the tube of her roll-up, checked the burning end, and squinted at the mountain through the smoke. She had a gold tooth, which showed when she laughed, shaking her head and saying, '*Putain! Putain de merde!*'

We went back inside the room, where the table was magnificently laid. During the meal Luc's mother floated between the table and the kitchen on a cloud of maternal joy. Luc was looking so beautiful I could hardly eat my lobster. A photograph of the day shows me looking like an overweight schoolgirl, sucking the claw of a lobster in an underconfident way. At one point I dropped my napkin; I was glad to duck out of the conversation for a while. Everyone over fifty kept saying, 'What's she saying?' every time I opened my mouth. Brigitte and Georges were not speaking, not to each other nor to anybody else, but were both bent over their plates like they'd lost something in the salad. As I got down to table-leg level and scrambled for my napkin, I saw their hands, tightly gripped together, like those of people desperate in prayer, two white vegetable tubers, entwined.

The painter uncle was there in his candy-blue jumper, a tiny, virile celibate who always grinned as he talked. I don't know what Luc had done, or failed to do, to his teeth. He had a little receding chin and his skin was nut brown, like Luc's. In temperament he had none of Luc's sweetness, though Luc had some of his tortuous sourness. He, too, had been imprisoned in the POW camp with his brother and Monsieur Desarthes. At one time, in the Fifties, he had been quite a well-known painter. He lived in the same huge house as Luc's parents, the former postmistress's house. It was vast, on three floors, and the way from the second up to the third was via a spiral staircase which was six metres in diameter. Light came in through a glass dome in the roof, and on the upper gallery many of the uncle's paintings were hung. I'd seen him groping his way round the spiral staircase under the huge dome, tittering to himself like a vain but lonely parrot nobody has taught any new words to for years. At lunch he told a story about a cousin on Luc's mother's side who was under the delusion that he was a spy on an important and highly secret assignment during the war. He would wake up in the night and go round knocking on strangers' doors, apologizing for having failed to accomplish his mission and for having given all the secrets away to the Germans. Luc's mother blushed softly for her cousin.

'There's always one in every family,' she said, and there was a silence during which each member of the family pinned the tail on one of the others.

While we were eating slices of a baguette-shaped piece of filo pastry, from which custard leaked at one end, which Luc's mother told me was called the curate's prick – 'The bishop's prick,' sniggered the uncle when he saw the size of it – two emaciated kittens arrived at the French windows, scratching at the glass. Luc's mother leaped up and rushed into the kitchen, holding the oven glove to her face.

Luc said angrily to his brother, 'Why have you got all these cats? Why didn't you drown them? They're starving. It's worse for them if you're sentimental.'

'They keep the rats down.'

'Rubbish.'

Later that day we saw Georges stalking over to his barn with a shotgun. Over the following hour we heard one shot, then two, then a silence, the banging of a barn door, a scuffle and more shots. No-one dared come out till it was over. 'Happy now?' Georges asked that evening when we passed him on the road.

That spring Georges took the train up to Paris for the first time in fifteen years to go and see Marcel.

'I need help,' he said. 'My wife is a whore. It is driving me mad.'

Marcel replied, 'But I can only help those with delusions. Suppose we reconstruct the sentence.'

'How?'

'We invert it,' Marcel said. 'I am mad – pause – and my wife is a whore.'

Georges referred to Marcel from then on as *l'alcoolique*, as though even if he had been one he was the only one in the world.

One night – maybe he was high on the new crop of marijuana – Georges trashed Brigitte's dairy. I was writing in the room above, and my heart bolted and crashed into my ribcage as the first milk churn hit the stone floor. It was a waste, because they'd paid good money, earned leek by leek, carrot by carrot, equipping the dairy to conform to European standards the previous winter.

Three months later he threw Brigitte out on a charge of multiple adultery. He didn't wait for the private detective's report, which said she really *had* been visiting her mother in Marseilles at Pentecost. So she left. An intelligent woman, a qualified rheumatologist who had spent twenty years, childless, on that mountain, planting and harvesting leeks and carrots, and playing the third Schubert impromptu on her childhood piano, which was as flat as a punctured tyre, but we didn't notice because we had nothing to compare it to until, one day, my own piano arrived.

She took nothing with her except a few personal possessions and the little Renault 4 they'd used to transport the milk churns. Watching her drive away, Georges picked up the phone, rang the insurance broker and cancelled her car insurance from that minute of that hour. She later moved in with the butcher who worked behind the counter at the supermarket, a big hairy man who kept goats for a hobby. Whenever she met me in the street she would ask casually after the family, squeeze my hand and tell me to look out for myself.

4. Local Life

Siesta

Afternoon, summer. A shallow sweep of wind blurring the grass – a casual gesture, a woman ruffling her lover's hair, for no reason. The space, the scent – of tobacco, leather, paints and mouthwash – in the bed, left by the man who seems like the only man alive, to me; the one with the halo round his head in a crowd, if I should ever see him in a crowd. The light is diffused by a scrap of curtain pinned to the door frame, a snatch of red cotton, tinting the room to the shade of my inner eyelids, so it still seems like a room in one of my dreams. Here I am again, awake, walls buckling, flies by my head on the pillow. His riding boots kicked off by the bed, his blue check shirt and leather hat on the pegs jammed into the wall, a photo of the horses, the dark armoire, the frolicsome bishop's starched white linen, stacked like stationery, interleaved with brittle relics, spidery grey rosemary and lavender, pressed flat, without scent.

He sleeps with his body, flinging himself down, exhausted, out of sheer need, as a horse drinks from a stream, thirstily, till he's had enough. Then he slips from the bed like a little Red Indian boy, fresh and stealthy; just the clink of his belt as he does up his jeans before stepping outside into the hot metal air. The dog hoists herself to her feet, still asleep, and bustles noisily across the room after him. I hear him talking to her outside as he carries out some small task, polishing a bridle or knocking a nail into the wall, little phrases, murmurs, up, down, round about, short, longer, tender. The words themselves have dropped away like the outer case of a nut, leaving only the sweet, soft inner sounds he keeps back for her. Good dog. She is smug as hell. I don't want to hurt her, or get rid of her. I just want to be able to say, in clear words she will understand, 'Look, I'm his girlfriend, OK. You're his dog.'

He had made his own bed, like Odysseus, the winter before we met, from the logs of a lightning tree, and laid on the frame a mattress as dense as peat. I sang him the song I'd learned in primary school about the lightning tree. He liked it and said they hadn't had singing at the school in the village, only '*des chansons cathos*' – religious dirges. The fact that we had sat cross-legged on the floor singing about 'down by the river when the wind blows free, there's a whisper of green on the lightning tree' made him think England was a country where pagan rituals and stories about the regeneration of the earth occupied a large part of the school curriculum. When he'd finished the lightning bed he phoned Gigi, who came up to inspect it.

'*On essaie?*' she had asked, understandably, since she hadn't driven seven kilometres up the mountain just to look at a bed. He said she had been about to kick off her shoes when he'd stopped her. 'Sorry,' he'd said, holding her back. 'It's reserved.'

'For *who*?'

He'd shrugged. 'The one who'll turn up in the spring.'

'*Salaud*,' she'd said, coldly, and left.

They didn't speak for another two months, till some weeks after Luc and I met. I couldn't work out why she ignored me. I'd walk past her dress shop and she'd stare glassily out, through me, as though I were the mannequin and she the browsing customer who saw nothing that impressed her. When we first talked properly, at a party, she had just had her hair cut short and dyed pale auburn.

'You've never cut your hair short?' she asked me gently.

'No.'

'You will,' she said. 'Just wait.' She was solicitous about my new life. Was I enjoying the farm? Was the country air suiting me? She might as well have asked straight out 'Good orgasms, *chérie*?' and had done with it.

'Charming, isn't she?' Luc said smoothly after she'd slid away again. They were rather well suited to each other.

'She's OK. Wasn't she blond last week?'

'She was.'

'What's her natural colour?'

'Green.'

The bed was solid. To remove it from the room he would have had to chop it back up into pieces again. On the wall behind the bed he had drawn a giant fantasy insect. His bed, the walls, his voice, paper, stone, scissors . . . I fell backwards into sleep. I dreamed of other houses, other beds. In my dreams Luc lived in all these other houses, too, even on the Seventies housing estate where I'd spent my childhood. I'd go and fetch myself some orange squash from the cupboard in the break between children's TV and homework, and Luc would be there in the garden, sitting on the climbing frame, swinging his legs. I woke and he was sitting back on the bed again, smiling. He had eyes like burnished coins in a fountain, and his face was dark golden brown, too, with steel-grey hair, too old for his young face and adolescent frame.

'You look nice,' I said sleepily.

There was a huge gilt-framed mirror by the bed, purloined from the bishop's bedroom. I'd carried it across from the summer house with Henri, the cardiologist who wrote pornographic stories. I read them for him and sent them back to him at his surgery with textual criticism, which raised his non-professional standing with his secretary no end. Henri was divorced, bored and had a new passion every month – water-skiing, motorbiking, sailing, hang-gliding, playing the trombone. It didn't matter what it was as long as it involved a large piece of equipment. Every time he acquired a new piece of equipment he also acquired a new girlfriend to go with it. When the enthusiasm was over, he'd write an erotic story involving the equipment, the girl and the latest sexual fantasy. This allowed his friends, who might otherwise have been bewildered by the turnover, to index the episodes of his life accordingly, with three simple code words, e.g., trombone, Alice, seaweed. While we'd carried the mirror, Luc had been on horseback, giving instructions about flower beds and ruts in the path, dodging back out of view of the mirror in case the horse saw its own reflection, shied and crashed into the mirror, leaving glass on the tracks. 'Bad for the tyres,' Luc said. He was never superstitious about normal things. Mirrors and ladders held no fears at all for Luc.

He looked fondly at himself, at me looking at him, in the mirror.

'*C'est vrai. Je suis très beau,*' he agreed.

We both looked back at me. I wasn't brown or thin enough. He himself corresponded more closely than I did to what he described as his type. I think he believed that if he assured me and others often enough that I wasn't the kind of woman he usually went for, he would eventually be able to say, quoting one of the two lines from Proust everyone in France knows, 'To think that I have ruined my life for a woman who wasn't even my type.'

'Never mind, *coquine*. You'll get better-looking every day you spend with me. By the time we split up you'll be a beauty. Come, get up. There's someone here to see you.'

'In a minute.'

He threw my jeans onto the bed. 'Wear those, or Stefan will go looking up your skirt.'

I lay there a bit longer, so as not to just do what he said, watching daddy-long-legs lollop across the grubby ceiling with their langlauf strides. A quick glance round, then they'd disappear up a crack in the ceiling. Above was a room full of books, Luc's collection. Biographies of James Dean and Jimi Hendrix, books on Matisse and dreams, art books, portfolios of lithographs tied with ribbon, translations of Goethe and Shakespeare, and dust everywhere, on the shelves, the books, the pictures and the floor. I was often surprised at the things he'd read.

'I read *Hamlet* once,' he told me. 'It's a cracker. There's a dog in it.'

Was there? 'Are you sure?'

'Oh, yes,' he said. 'He's in a boat and they're escaping across a lake. There's a soliloquy; he's talking to the dog.'

He also loved the novels of Cormac McCarthy, because there were horses in them. But most of the shelves were taken up with Buddhist texts. He read them slowly, word for word, by the fire after dark, or on the terrace on his day off, his feet up on the wall and his hair growing hot under a decomposing Huck Finn hat, treating them like comic novels, reading out the good bits – not mocking, but full of admiration for their sly brand of tranquillity.

'*Ecoute*: "A mandarin loved a courtesan. 'I will be yours', she told him, 'when you have spent one hundred nights waiting for me, sitting on a stool in my garden, beneath my window.' But on the ninety-ninth night the mandarin stood up, tucked his stool under his arm and went away."'

'And?' Who cared? I didn't like the would-be bathetic tone of these mini-narratives. I'd grown up with the epigrammatic style in advertising slogans. Lao Tse and co. sounded like fortune-cookie writers or lyricists to me. I just wasn't of an Oriental cast of mind. I operated on the vertical, not the horizontal axis, I thought, getting out of bed and putting on my jeans. I preferred Jesus, because he was sweaty and young and had lots of friends and got into trouble. And he wasn't a writer. It made his words seem more trustworthy, in the long run.

Out on the terrace my feet burned on the brick tiles. Even sluggish with sleep you still had to run. I came to the stone arch below the dairy and stopped to lay my hand on the horse and feel the reassurance of his coarse black coat. He stood in silence against the cool wall, a dark, uncomplicated shape, passing the time, waiting for his ninety-ninth day.

Stefan and Luc were sitting on the lawn under the lime tree at a table. Luc introduced me: '*mon copain*,' he said. 'Stefan.' A small, handsome, fit man, functional looking, like something you could buy in an ironmonger's.

'Ah. *L'Anglaise. Salut*,' he said.

Luc said afterwards, 'He's cross because I found you first. He goes all round the countryside, cycling, running, climbing, stays up late talking, drives to cafés, goes to the cinema, plays with his politician friends, hangs out in jazz clubs and he never meets a better woman than his wife. And I just sit and wait and you turn up.'

'What do you write?' Stefan asked.

('He reads everything.')

I said I'd written a novel, and was writing another one.

'Is it in French?' he wanted to know. 'Can I read it?'

'No,' I said, 'you can't. It's a foreigner's perk. No-one you meet can read what you've written.' It was true, and went with not having a pedigree or an accent any-one could trace.

Stefan said, 'She's secretive.'

Luc said, 'Maybe she just isn't any good.'

We went down to the barn to look at Luc's paintings, the ones he'd done since the spring. We stopped on the way to squeeze the fruit. Up at the summer house, Luc's parents were sitting out on the terrace in high-backed wicker chairs. They looked as though they were posing for the image we'd remember them by when they were dead. His mother counted the days we were together. Two months now and no sign of a rift. 'Is it serious, then?' asked her cousin, the wife of the mayor. His mother thought it was. 'But she's English,' said her cousin. '*Elle n'est pas d'ici.*'

'Ah well,' Luc told me his mother replied, 'if it's the best he can do . . . It's time he was married again. Doesn't want to be too old to be a father. If she makes him happy . . .'

Inside the barn the two latest paintings were spread out to dry on the cement floor. Luc sat in a mottled armchair, upholstered in dark-red velvet, at the far end of the room. Part of the roof had been replaced with glass, and a soft swoop of muslin billowed like a cradle, where a ceiling might have been. The dog lay in the straw bales in the corner. Stefan couldn't keep still and kept picking up pots and rolls of tape. He had taken up painting himself recently, and Luc had 'passed him' a show, one he didn't want to do himself, in a tourist village on the coast. He said that while preparing the show Stefan took on the whole persona of 'the Painter', which, as even Luc, who was not a great reader of existential texts, could tell you, was an article of Sartrean bad faith. Luc had even lent him a studio, further up the valley, between villages. 'Sadly,' Luc said, after a careful pause, 'no-one turned up at the opening. Just him and the woman who runs the tourist office.'

'And he didn't even turn up at the opening,' Stefan told me. 'I think he was jealous. He likes to think he's the only painter around here.'

Luc was preparing an exhibition to be shown in Burgundy — 'wherever that is,' he said. At the far end of the room was a 100-metre roll of brown wrapping paper, which he gummed several times to itself and folded over to create a tough paper canvas. Then he diluted his paints down to a thin wash, took a kitchen broom and swept the paint over the surface. When an interviewer asked him on a television show why he painted on paper, Luc said, 'Because it's cheap.' Stefan was furious with him for saying that. 'He's a dentist!' he'd say. 'He drives a jeep!' Luc said Stefan was in no position to criticize, because Stefan lived off his wife.

'Girlfriend,' Stefan said.

'The mother of your child.'

'A woman I love.' Not 'the', I noticed.

'I bet you do,' Luc said, poking at a bale of straw with his toe. 'Where would you be without her? Who'd pay your bills?' What Luc really needed was a woman who'd bring home a wage cheque to keep him in paint.

Towards the end of the afternoon I shut down my computer and went to join them again. They were still talking.

'Stefan wants us to go and eat pizza with him on the coast.'

'Wonderful. I'd love to. Shall we set off right away?'

Luc said, 'Why would we want to do that?'

'Because we like pizza?'

He shrugged.

'Because we like the sea?'

'You see,' Stefan said. 'Luc?'

'Do what you want. I'm staying here.'

'You see?' Stefan said to me.

We walked as far as the road with him. He pulled his bike out of the rhododendrons by the gate and put on his baseball cap to cover his pate. Luc ran his fingers through his own luxurious hair and whistled softly to the horses, who turned, clocked him and began their listless progress through the field.

'Take care,' Luc told him seriously, his hand on Stefan's shoulder as he sat there with one foot balanced on the gate. He gave him a push, sending him whizzing off down the mountain road.

'*Allez, plus de pédale!*' Luc yelled after him. '*Allez*, faster! *Plus vite!*'

He'd be home in seven minutes. One minute per kilometre. Luc put his arm round me, so we looked just like a real couple waving goodbye at a gate, grinned happily and said in his little English voice that came from somewhere at the back of the class, 'Hurry hurry, everybody! Don't be late.'

Horses

He took me for a walk. The dog came, too. We arrived in the field by the green painted gate, where his two horses stood. They were huge as bronze monuments, scarcely moving, their flanks like continents on a map, their hooves like shires. They were beginning to shed their winter coats. As we approached, they froze and watched. Luc said, 'Do you want to ride?' I didn't know how. He passed me the rope bridle. 'Hold the buckles fast', he said, 'so they don't make a noise. Always show the back of your hand, not the palm. This one's Hector.'

Hector and Lux were his strange, adopted passion. He was not a natural horseman; he'd started late, and he had chosen these two, of an almost prehistoric Pyrenean breed, because they were strong and slow and seemed to be able to pick up harmonics from ancient volcanic movements inside the earth. They were his path away from himself, that part of himself he feared, which twitched and fluttered and could tip over in the wind. They were what he had turned to when he gave up sailing boats. He denied they bore any symbolic weight for him. They were the things themselves, not symbols; they were so prehistoric and atavistic they didn't need to stand for anything. They were at the end of the road, the deepest sound, the darkest night. They were the things first painted on the walls of caves, the things first represented.

Hector watched me coming, his huge, sullen eye as big as a stone. Luc was rolling a cigarette. The dog was sitting by him. I tried to empty my head of fear, unlocking the muscles in my face, and concentrated on accepting this huge animal and not being afraid. As I came up close to him I breathed very gently and lightly, and I felt a humming sensation run through my body, deep down. I felt my senses lift, so that the horse was wrapped in something coming from me, a prayer. Right up against him, so I could smell the straw on him and the sweet dung stuck to his tail. I slipped the bridle over his head, touched his ears and buckled it quickly under his chin. I hadn't done up a buckle since primary school. Taking the rope, I led him back to Luc.

Luc was convinced then that I would ride like a dream, that it wouldn't matter that I was English and blonde – not his type at all – that I wrote at a computer, kept my make-up in the bathroom and was afraid of rats. He would teach me, and together we'd act out his dream of a life, in slow motion, tethered only to the course of the sun and straitened by paths through the forest.

We tied up the horses on iron hooks embedded in the wall outside the kitchen, and he took me into the tack room to fetch the brushes and blankets and pieces of complicated-looking leather gear. The process of saddling up a horse became familiar over the next few years, and I grew to love it, each buckle in its order, the deft, neat movements, the slot of leather through metal, and the terrifying moment when you slicked back his mouth with your forefinger to place the bit behind his yellow teeth. It reminded me of threading a sewing machine, which was something that came so unnaturally that once you'd learned the procedure it was impossible ever to forget or do differently from how you'd been taught.

In summer, fat, feasted flies stuck to their flesh like leeches and you had to flick them away, hoping that the irritation wouldn't make the horse kick or jump. Whenever you passed behind a horse, where it couldn't see you, you had to run your hand over the swell of its buttocks, so it knew where you were and wouldn't be frightened. This was so much second nature to Luc that sometimes he'd do it to me as I sat reading in the evening, just run his hand over my head as he passed.

During the preparations, though, every consideration was for the horse. For Luc it was quite clear: humans were perverted and complicated and had invented the world. To get on with a horse you had to start thinking and feeling from scratch, and if you did something wrong the horse was quite within its rights to lash out at you. Even if an animal, or one of its ancestors – 100 years ago, or back in the middle ages, or even back in that cave when it had all started to go wrong – had learned to be afraid at the hands of some previous owner, or car driver, or idiot farmer you'd never met, you had to live with that and accept you were part of a fallen species who deserved to get kicked or chomped. Stefan despised this primitive approach to horses, to the world. The world is complicated, he said, the more complicated the better – a troubled skein spun by the minds of men. It was Luc's Platonic view of the world that Stefan warned me of later, angrily rattling a step ladder as I stood on the topmost rung: 'He doesn't want you to go and live with him, he wants you to go and die with him! Get that into your head, *enfin, ma belle.*'

We finished brushing the horses and went inside to change. Luc found me a woollen jumper his mother had knitted for him, and we both wore jeans. He wore a leather jerkin with pockets for a knife, his tobacco, matches, a torch and quince jelly, pressed into a slab, for energy. Wrapped up for warmth, we ate our lunch on the terrace, plain white rice, with a fried egg each and some salad leaves. For months that was almost all we ate, because it was simple and Luc liked everything simple. In the evening we drank red wine with it, and sometimes a hunk of red meat, or a chicken bought ready-roasted from the market. He would sometimes enjoy the dishes I made, fish stews and huge salads, but I knew that things were rocky whenever he stalked in at meal time and threw half a packet of rice into a pan of boiling water.

After we'd given the horses some hay, we hawked the saddles out of the tack room. Luc liked Arabian saddles, heavy as nineteenth-century furniture, the kind of thing a pope would sit on to evacuate his bowels, but with a pommel, a large, reinforced protuberance at the front, which stabbed you in the groin if the horse came to a sudden halt and sent you hurtling forwards over its ears. I staggered under the weight of it, my legs jammed right up into my pelvic sockets, but you had to lift it above the horse's back and lower it very gently, so it would barely register the moment of contact. Then you smartly lifted its tail, revealing the hole you had previously cleaned with a tough bristled brush, and wrapped *la croupe* round the root of the tail, buckling it into place to stop the saddle sliding when you were riding steep slopes. Luc checked my work at every step, but never told me what to do, so everything had to be worked out from first principles. That way, he said, you understand what it is you're doing.

Once I'd got up on the horse and got over my vertigo we set off, walking slowly down the field, past the house, through long grass, till we reached a small stream in the forest. The water was completely transparent, visible only as a thinning of the light and a movement over stones. Over our heads the branches creaked and rustled, set off by the parting of the lower branches as the horses brushed against them. Luc rode ahead of me, occasionally snapping off a branch with a quick, fierce gesture to clear the way for me, and for himself on the way home. We climbed a hill through the chestnut forests on the other side of the stream, and then down again, through waist-high bracken, till we came to a track the colour of pencil shavings, where the horses turned left and began to trot.

I didn't fall off. We never cantered for long because Luc always wanted to spare the horses. We stopped for breath on the top of a gentle hill, just beyond some bee-hives, and when we looked back to where we'd come from we could see the farm. Georges had lit a fire. We hoped he wasn't smoking Brigitte's body over the heat, curing her.

We never talked much on these rides. Occasionally I'd shout, 'Wait!' as I tried to wrestle Hector's head up out of a bouquet of young leaves. He never took much notice of me as I yanked at his head. Luc would turn round in the saddle, his reins wrapped loosely round the pommel, and say, 'Gently. *Doucement. Fais gaffe.*'

For him, riding was all about communion and harmony, and I liked the excitement, the thrill. I liked to feel I was riding the horse. For that I needed to be hurtling across country, with the horse reaching out with great strides and my body moving with his, like a piston. When I learned to go out on my own, I sometimes had to stop and rub him down with leaves, scrape away the white foam oozing from his flanks and his neck and walk him slowly home.

I wasn't always kind to the horse. Often I was angry

114

with him, because after that first day he realized that, even though I may have had some folk memory of being at home on a horse, he could feel the weight of my city sensibilities, the gestures of someone used to driving a car, or having full control. Neither of Luc's horses had been trained, and they would probably have been quite dangerous to ride if they hadn't been so laid-back in temperament. They knew the mountains so well, there was never a path they hadn't seen before, so there wasn't much you had to do, just keep in the saddle and decide if you were going to walk, trot or canter, and even that usually went with the terrain. Most of the time we walked, especially in the evening, by moonlight, over the crags, returning from the eleventh-century monastery on the other side of the border, exhausted, watchful of the weather, hungry again. I watched him ride ahead of me, his hips swaying very slightly, occasionally saying a word or two to the dog, who ran with him, and his straight back and lean thighs, and felt a mixture of love and impatience. I could either be there or not be there. I knew he'd carry on doing the same things if I left. He'd say, in the end it's all the same. You do what you want.

Walking home along the crest of the mountain, through the smoky dusk and down the dark forest paths, I sometimes thought of Angus, who was married to one of my friends. He'd been working in a London theatre in the Seventies. He was in bed one night when the phone rang. A friend asked him to collect a spare part from an address in south London and drive through the night with it to a place in France he'd never been. He drove to the port, crossed the Channel and arrived before dawn at the black edge of a canal. He stopped the engine, got out of the car, stretched and smelled the foggy air and said to himself, in surprise, 'This is it; this is my place.'

If you are lucky enough to find your place, he said, to sniff the air and know you have something to do there, then you are lucky in love.

Estranged from Luc, sitting in Angus's kitchen, drinking the wine he'd made, which was not Burgundy because he hadn't been able to stay in the place he loved, nor with the woman he'd met there, I reminded him of what he'd said. 'You didn't listen,' he said. 'I told you, if you find your place you should never actually live in it, never make it your home. In the same way,' he said kindly, giving me his hand, unwanted because it wasn't the hand of the man I loved, not Luc's, though its shape and the feel of it under my fingers were almost the same, 'never live with the man you think you cannot live without. And make sure you never do both.'

Stefan

Stefan cultivated me as fastidiously as if I'd been a political contact. He had been brought up in Normandy and sent to school in Paris because he was clever. At sixteen he had helped lead the *lycéens* in revolt during May 1968, and had drunk coffee with Beauvoir and Sartre.

'Drunk coffee?' I said, rather scornfully.

'There was a lot to discuss. Of course we drank coffee. You sound like a communist,' he said.

By June of that year he was a card-carrying Maoist, and his girlfriend, one of the student teachers at his school, went with him round factories close to Paris and Lyons, trying to drum up revolutionary fervour among the workers. They were part of a cell network, which at that time meant you were a revolutionary with underground links all over Europe. They spent a lot of time making posters and having sex. He was first imprisoned at seventeen for throwing stones. Later, while working on factory production lines, he would be sent down for inciting the workers to strike and creating riots. He was never actually arrested for direct political incitement, he said, there was always some other trumped-up charge, like stealing or damaging machinery.

When the revolution sputtered in the late Seventies,

he did a stint as the food critic on *Libération*, then ran his restaurant on the beach at Gruissan. He claimed that Jacques Lang, the minister for culture in the 1980s, had offered him the position of minister for rock and roll, but that he'd turned it down. One day he arrived in the village and decided to stay. He said it felt truly democratic, and he liked living close to a border. He also liked living in the cobbled Rue de la République because, he said, in summer everyone kept their windows open and you could hear a concert of copulating couples being relayed gently out into the night. After all, he said, what else is there to do after midnight in a place like this?

He said that doing nothing all day – his partner worked – was a way of showing solidarity with the unemployed, of sharing their burden, which was not so much one of poverty, though there was that, as one of having no social status. He threw himself into sport – he ran, cycled, rode, swam and played tennis, teaching the children of the village for free – tennis being a suitable weapon in the armoury of the potential *épateur de la bourgeoisie*, involving, as it did, beating them roundly at their own game. He was fiercely competitive for a Maoist, and his body, which must once have been puny, had been built up to something highly sprung and muscled. He had the best legs and the best tan in the village, though this was slightly offset by his having steel hair round the edges with a bald dome on top.

He often came and hung around in my flat at the beginning of the afternoon, between the end of *Panorama*, a rather difficult-to-follow cultural discussion programme that goes out on the radio at midday, and two o'clock, when he would go off to see one of his mistresses, who lived a few doors up, saying, 'I just come round here first to warm up.' She was

German, looked like a former high-jump champion and strode around the village with two straining grey-hounds crossed with something wolflike for extra size on the end of a leash.

He had a thing about German women. The village was twinned with a town of equivalent size in Germany, and Stefan had a seat on the twinning com-mittee. The year before he'd taken a group of children from the lycée on an exchange to Germany. One of the German mothers had been flame-haired and hot for him, and he'd spent the final night with her in the back of her VW. Shortly afterwards she had written a letter on pink paper with a floral border to say she planned to spend the summer in the village, so they wouldn't be apart for long. He had been quite looking forward to some varied sex and an opportunity to practise his German, but when he received her letter he said his sperm ran cold. Aside from the cloying message, which seemed to him particularly repellent in her language, though he wasn't a prejudiced man, she had enclosed a present, wrapped in tissue and scented with her perfume. He said it was the kind of perfume you could tell had been made in a factory, in great vats. He said real French perfume, the kind Gigi and her friends wore, smelled as though it had been made in tiny phials. In the same way, a small sip of wine tasted entirely different to a great gulp. This was part of his political theory – to do with the microcosm not being necessarily identical to the macrocosm. When Stefan unwrapped the present, he was horrified to find a photograph of the German woman herself with no clothes on, lying in a field of long grass, in a frame upholstered with floral fabric. There was something about the package that was utterly opposed to his whole notion of sex and freedom and honesty. She had packaged herself for him. He decided he'd rather have the exile with her long nose and loping dogs than a luscious flame-haired beauty with her legs spread provocatively in a field.

Stefan once tried to seduce Gigi by hiding in a cupboard in her shop, *à la Tartuffe*, but she threw him out into the street. '*Elle m'a foutu sur le cul!*' – 'I landed on my arse!' he shouted. The problem was, Gigi explained to him a long time after, that he had leaped *out* at her, flinging himself into her arms. He just didn't have a clue, she said. Now Luc, on the other hand, would have hidden himself in the cupboard and stubbornly refused to come out, until you felt it was your fault he was in the cupboard and you'd better get in there with him.

Sometimes Stefan read to me. My favourite passage, the one I've remembered, involved a girl and boy in their mid to late teens walking up one of those staircases from landing to landing to the top of an apartment block in Paris. The girl is walking ahead, a few steps higher than the boy. There is silence between them, only the sound of their feet. Then she says, 'Can you see my knickers?' There is a long pause. After several more steps and the turn of the staircase he says, 'Yes, I can.' She replies at the next turn of the stair. 'What colour are they, then?' He pauses, thinks, pauses, then says, 'They're blue.'

Stefan thought this was the most erotic passage he had ever read in a book. He said it was obvious, if you thought about it. The boy can't see her knickers, she knows he can't, but he says he can to please her, to please himself. She asks what colour they are anyway, authorizing him to say whatever he likes, letting him know that when they reach the top apartment they will make love, and he says quietly, they are blue, avoiding the pornographic, leaving it still open, enigmatic, so she can still decide to send him off after a cool tisane.

I hadn't understood this at all, and I don't think it's what the author meant, but Stefan's exegesis was erotic in its own way, and I'm sure the author would have been pleased.

Stefan was much better than the radio. He could talk for hours on end about sex, and the government, and about the Super-Gigis he'd met when he went up to Paris to ask Yves St Laurent to finance his emergency food trip to Gdansk in 1982. He said he could love a woman for just one tiny detail. He loved the German woman two doors up because she always smiled with such a look of lascivious relish as she bent to kiss him. Stefan is more fun than most people, but he has an inflated sense of how much people want him – women and the police in particular. He justifies his political inactivity – *activiste à la retraite* – by saying he is still wanted by the international police for kidnapping a judge in Toulouse in 1974. It turned out they got the wrong judge, and kept his liberal homonym trussed up in the back of a van for ten days. Stefan had to flee to Italy to be hidden by the Red Brigade. They stopped looking for him after a couple of weeks, though. 'They just didn't want you enough,' I said. In the car we used to listen to Pulp, which he pronounced Poulpe, like an octopus. I told him Jarvis Cocker was working class, but then his daughter brought a picture of him home from school, and Stefan came round to contest my notion of working class, waving the picture of Jarvis, pouting in tight trousers with a hint of tint on his lips on a bed in a Paris hotel, photographed by Bettina Rheims.

Because Luc wouldn't go anywhere, Stefan took me for drives in the afternoon, into Spain, to the coast at Calella, or to La Bisbal or Figueras, where we visited the Dali museum with our noses in the air. Or Cadaqués, blue and white, like friendly china. He said,

'The north of a southern country is far more northern than the south of a northern country,' and you only had to drive over the border to see it was true. Where we lived was deep southern country, and the stone was rose-pink and warm, the vegetation dry and coastal. In certain parts of northern Spain, only a few miles to the south, you felt you had travelled far north into industrial Catalunia.

We drank cold beer in high ceilinged bars where I was the only woman, or strolled down the *ramblas*, past huge, grey modernist buildings. Cafés and sex were his two favourite pressure points for taking the pulse of a country. If he heard a new café had opened in Figueras he would go there and deconstruct the bar stools, the juke box, the coy murals, the range of bottles behind the bar, the age group aimed at, and what you could learn from that about the social and economic condition of the town. We ate complex meals of tapas, or Chinese food, with flavours wrapped up together, indissoluble, and sauces that no amount of chemistry could ever have separated back to their constituent parts. We'd argue about John Berger's interpretation of Spain in his book on Picasso, that the only kind of revolution they could have had was one based on a belief in the possibility of apotheosis – that everything could be magically transformed overnight. 'No wonder you like him,' he said. 'That's what you think, too.' Berger argued that Picasso had remained a typical Spaniard all his life, constantly overhauling himself and looking for a radical change, almost religious in his belief that the world could change by some other means than the slow, methodical, carefully programmed Marxist method. Look at him when he joined the communist party, he says. Imagine the power he had as one of the world's most famous men. He could have done anything! Why wasn't he out there as an ambassador, or even an activist himself? All he did was design them a lousy symbol, a dove. Put like that it did seem rather meagre, though I felt Berger and Stefan were expecting too much of the wrong man.

It was the kind of thing we argued over, driving, or walking down a beach on winter afternoons. One day, as we crossed the border back into France and Stefan had gone through the ritual of ducking the sleeping border guards, he said, 'We are lucky in France. All the best love songs are in a foreign language. We keep ourselves pure by not knowing any of those words. And anyway,' he added, 'it's a bit ridiculous in your language, the way they're always saying "I love you". At least in French it's ambiguous. You might only be saying, "I like you." Then a bit later, looking out of the window as the Canigou appeared on our right and we were nearly home, he said thoughtfully, in a voice expressing nothing but pleasure at being there, alive, in the car driving back from Spain in the early evening: '*Je suis plein d'amour. Je suis plein d'amour.*'

Elections

Luc had been told by one of his patients that his astrological chart for what was left of the year was not all that promising, but that the following year he would be able to do whatever he wanted with success. Stefan sourly suggested he might like to stand for mayor.

The village was run at the time by a *député-maire*, a mayor who was also the local parliamentary representative in Paris. He was a slight man in his fifties. He had been born in the village and was married to one of Luc's mother's cousins. He was a good socialist in a socialist community, but he had grown slack and accustomed to power. Up for re-election, he had snubbed the local *pétanque* team, most of them communists, Spanish refugees and civil-war veterans. They invited him to a *vin d'honneur* two nights before the election. He went to a dinner party given by Gigi instead. They reacted quickly, rounded up the vote and decided to go for the other side.

The other side was represented by a man called Subleyras, a stocky man, with arms that looked as though he knew what a ploughshare was, and hands that dangled and almost grazed the ground. His father had been mayor in the Fifties. Before that he had run an ironmonger's shop in the Rue St Florian, and used to store up Picasso's canvases for safe-keeping in the room at the back of the shop. This often came up in the son's speeches.

Subleyras was the perfect populist. Unlike the mayor, he knew the value of sitting on the terrace of the café late at night and catching people in conversation. His conversation was crude and macho. He talked about '*propreté*', which he appeared to be using in the sense of keeping the streets clean, but which had darker resonances for the very few Arabs in the village. He promised work in traditional village occupations.

After the devastating first round, which Subleyras won by a large majority, the old mayor had a week to rally support before the second vote. At meetings in the *salle de Spectacle*, promises were made regarding international *pétanque* tournaments, a covered swimming pool, the conversion of the big empty house with the sixteenth-century façade opposite Luc's surgery into a museum for local crafts – espadrille-making, corks, fabrics. The regionalist agenda of the 1960s rebels had been effectively hijacked by the Nineties right. The second day of voting came round. Mitterrand sent a telegram of support, but Subleyras won by sixty-two votes.

Within two days the outgoing mayor had raised a formal complaint. One of the new mayor's henchmen had been seen distributing tracts in the market place on the day before the election – elections are held on Sundays in France. No publicity is allowed during the twenty-four-hour period before an election. A request for a re-vote had been formally lodged with the Ministry of the Interior.

The new mayor got on with the job, as the newly elect, with mock humility, like to say. He threw out the champagne socialists and cancelled an exhibition of Picasso's graphics at the museum because it was too expensive a project and would be better done by a museum up in Paris. Instead he proposed an exhibition of all the museum's holdings by local artists. Many artists withdrew their work from the permanent collection because they didn't want their 'eels in plastic tunnel' displayed anywhere near Madame Leblanc's meditation in pastels on the cherry orchards in bloom. War was declared. The village had always lived peacefully till then, but that year was the most turbulent in its history. Divisions ran through families and trades unions, siblings stopped speaking, people threw their neighbours' horses out of their fields. The new mayor rollicked through the streets at the Saturday market, arm in arm with his deputies, hugging people, kissing small animals and ordering everybody drinks. He got so much into the spirit of things he began to overspend.

One night, while dining at Le Jardin Fleuri, he discovered Johnny Hallyday's manager was sitting at the adjacent table. Johnny Hallyday must be nearly sixty now. He wears a leather jacket and rides a Harley-Davidson. He sings. He tours. He has about seventy electricians and nine hairdressers and several ex-wives, and they all come too. He plays in big places like Montpellier and Toulouse – it helps if they have a large population of OAPs. The mayor brought the manager over to his table, got talking and decided it would be a good idea if Johnny brought his act to the village the following September, instead of the Slovenian baroque ensemble from Ljubljana. It was an act of bravado. No word had yet arrived from the Ministry of the Interior on the question of the re-election. They were due to report back by June. If there was a need for a new election and Subleyras won it, vindicating his earlier victory, he'd still be in power by the time Johnny came to town, and would make a huge financial success of the concert. Failing that, he could always raise the money from local industrialists, or sell off a Matisse. Likewise if there was no re-election. But if there was one, and he lost, the returning mayor would find himself footing the bill for the concert that was estimated at something completely crazy like seven million francs. The local industrialists wouldn't support him, and since he was a supporter of the museum and its 'elitist' policies, he couldn't possibly think of selling a Matisse. It was very confusing the way the right-wing candidate was always accusing the socialist of elitism, and the socialist accused the right-winger of pandering to the masses.

From the moment the pact between manager and mayor was sealed, the village was plastered with posters. Johnny was the word on everybody's lips. The teenagers were furious, and held a demonstration, supported by their teachers, who hadn't been on a good demo since 1974. They wanted Jarvis Cocker and I was with them on that one, but nothing would move the mayor.

One Friday evening in May, a year after the election, a message arrived from the Ministry of the Interior. The minister considered the election had indeed been unfairly influenced against the outgoing incumbent by the distribution of tracts in the market place on the morning of the day before the ballot. No-one really believed this, but those who stood to gain from the judgement read the reprieve as a kind of moral arrangement of the political tea leaves. It was as good as if it had been true. The two sides took up their positions. This time there was to be only one vote. Everything would be decided in a day.

Luc would occasionally sit and chat with Subleyras on the terrace of the right-wing café. 'He's my patient,' he'd say, 'I like talking to him. He bought a painting off me once. It doesn't mean I'm going to vote for him.'

'You shouldn't talk to him like that if you're not. Everyone else thinks you're on his side.'

'And you care about that? It's nothing to do with you. You haven't even got a vote. I don't know why you're getting so involved.'

'I am involved. He hates foreigners!'

'Is that what Stefan says?'

'Yes. But he's right.'

'You listen to Stefan too much.'

'Because he cares what happens outside the village.'

'And this is a *village* election.'

'Just don't be surprised if he shuts down the museum' – contemporary art was decadent, he said, which made Luc laugh – 'and puts your pictures up in the tourist information office.'

'Good idea,' Luc said. 'I'd be happy if there was nothing to do here. No museum. No Festival Méditerranéen, no Fête de la Sardane, none of that tourist stuff. Nothing for visitors at all.'

'You could always go on day trips to Toulon for entertainment.' Toulon was the centre of right-wing extremism along the coast, and had anti-Arab rallies like other towns have fêtes and whist drives.

'This is *local* politics. It's not about left and right, it's about the village.'

'Local politics is global politics.'

'Ah, yes, the global village,' he said. 'I wouldn't know about that. You'll have to talk to Stefan about that.'

'Anyway,' he said later when the point had had time to settle, 'you know I won't really vote for him. I don't know why you're getting so upset.'

'You won't?'

I was dropping him off outside the surgery, and he leaned down at the car window, 'Of course not. I'll vote for my mother's cousin's husband.'

*   *   *

Forty-eight hours before the election, Subleyras was to give his final public address. It had been an extraordinary week. Everyone had taken sides. Unbelievable alliances of convenience had been struck. Promises untenable and implausible had been made. The tennis club could look forward, in theory, to twelve new courts, to be constructed on the site of the old railway station, next door to the cherry co-operative. The question of the perspex roof for the swimming pool had been floated yet again. The director of the Museum of Modern Art had gone on sick leave. The mayor had targeted her as one of the ringleaders of the caviar-socialist set. In France, caviar, not champagne, indicates a love of luxury incompatible with socialist principles, since champagne, though still expensive, is something everyone should drink. She was hiding out in the restaurant run by her lover on the edge of the port, where there used to hang works donated by Picasso and Matisse in lieu of bar bills; they were eventually stolen, I've heard, so now there are only works by lesser painters, but it's still atmospheric and the fresh fish is good. Every now and then she slipped back to the village with a slightly deeper tan and dived into the dress shop, which the new mayor would never dare enter, since Gigi was a communist. The new mayor's problem was that, like most men in the village, he lusted painfully after both the director of the museum and Gigi, cultivated women both with beautiful skin, who for the last ten years had been running a sexual syndicate, sharing out Luc and a couple of other painters among them when they were between wealthy Parisian lovers.

The deposed mayor had held his meeting the previous evening. He had addressed a crowd of maybe 600 people, without passion, drily. The new mayor, defending his position, now took the stage by vaulting onto it, using his hand and wrist as a pivot. He'd hired a television crew from Toulouse, and they'd rigged up a huge Times Square-size screen behind him, so that as he walked up and down the stage with his microphone, looking remarkably school of Hallyday in gait, girth and general wolfishness, he was shown in close-up on the screen behind him. Not only could we watch his lips, we could see the spittle gather in the corners of his mouth. He strode up and down, and swung his hands about, and paused and swung again. I kept thinking he might break into a run, do a knife jump and start singing one of Barry Manilow's faster numbers. He talked, very smoothly, about how he wanted to run the town for the people, only for the people, and that meant, first of all, the people of the village, which meant people who had the births of four grandparents registered in the files at the *mairie*. He began to talk about the budget. He mentioned the plans and promises of his opponent. He crouched close to the edge of the stage. There was a rumour he had bribed someone to chuck their knickers at him – the woman who ran the crèche and was desperate to keep her job. I realized, appalled, that I was almost beginning to fancy him myself. I always went for slight men who looked like disgraced angels; he was big and sweaty, with a deep voice and a long stride, and I began to recognize in him a different kind of beauty, one that had beefy thighs and large hands and broad shoulders. He was so glad to be in his body, and had a kind of clumsy grace that made the rest of us feel small and Sunday-school neat. His face was creased and cracked with broken promises, like a cowboy's saddle. I realized the power of the demagogue could lie in sexiness, and not so much in straight sexiness but in that ability to make people fancy you against all their instincts. I could see how a meeting like this could really sway people; it was already starting.

Luc hadn't come to the meeting. He hated emotional circuses of any kind. Stefan was leaning against the wall at the end of a row. He was wearing a clean black T-shirt and jeans. He caught my eye, shook his head and pulled a face. I drifted off a bit, lulled by the rhetoric and the heat, and thinking how I liked the way Stefan always wore faded clean clothes, with that hint of having just showered and changed out of something extremely sweaty. I was still watching him when I saw him tense and then move forward, the way he did on the back line of the tennis court as I pushed a serve over towards him and he went in for the kill. The mayor had offered the microphone over for questions. Stefan twitched, though I knew he wouldn't speak. Someone else moved forward off the back wall and almost ran down the aisle, sprang up onto the stage, seized the microphone and started speaking. At first the crowd thought he must be speaking in support of Subleyras. He was clean-cut, young, handsome and well-dressed. Then his words began to surface like bubbles, popping in the listener's minds: 'disgrace', 'fascist', 'expenditure', 'Hallyday!', 'budget', 'mendacious', 'meretricious', 'racist', 'Le Pen', '*scandale*'. There was a snarl from the row behind me and the heavies got to their feet and pounded towards the stage. Meanwhile the mayor had forgotten he was on screen and was shown quivering with fury and loathing. The cameraman had frozen the shot, so the backdrop was of a hideous man in late middle age, with crazed eyes and hair bristling in his nostrils. The young man – who, it turned out, was in his first year at Nanterre, and whose mother had been kicked out of her job by the present mayor – was perfect. Before they could lynch him, he sprang off the stage, making the mayor's earlier leap, in retrospect, look gross and fake, and disappeared out of the back door. After that Subleyras never had a chance. I glanced over at Stefan, who was looking stunned. As we left he said, 'I was jealous. I have never been jealous before, it's against my political convictions to be jealous, but I was jealous of that young man for saying what I can no longer say.'

The old mayor won the election comfortably, and Subleyras stomped off over the hills and was scarcely seen again, as though, in some folk tale, a pinprick had entirely undone him, let the spirit out of him, so he was just a jumble of bones and flesh and sagging chins, and fine clothes that now flopped about his limbs but did not hide him. It is an extraordinary thing to do, to set oneself up for power, to invite the judgement of the crowd. Until the moment the outcome is announced you are high up, in the realm of the possible, of hope, even of desire; however unlikely you are to succeed, your very candidacy separates you from the rest. Afterwards, after failure, you slump back into the crowd, if you are lucky; but more often your aspiration has marked you in ways people cannot see, and you are never so able to feel like one of them as before you aspired to represent them. There is more disgrace, somehow, attached to the hubris of the man of power than to that of the lover, whom failure can even ennoble. I suppose it's because anyone can imagine losing in love, but very few people, far fewer than we imagine, are really interested in power.

In his role as the new mayor's nemesis, Johnny Hallyday probably came closer to political involvement than he'd ever been in his life, although his role was completely inadvertent. In the end the whole thing was decided by an act of God, who washed out the concert with rain, making an obscure Belgian singer into an obscure instrument of grace. Acts of God only seem to cover the weather. Imagine if your only instrument for expression of free will was the weather, if your only vindictive weapon was drizzle, or fog. No venomous letters, no cuckolding, no back-stabbing. It makes one less attracted to the idea of being God when there are so many more instruments of malice around for mere mortals to choose from.

Cherry Pie Project

Shortly before the cherries ripened, a month before the
May re-election, I was approached by a deputation
from the Foyer de Jeunesse, who are involved with
creating employment for the young and had a plan.
They needed me to supply a recipe for authentic
American cherry pie, which they would sell at the
Saturday morning market. We'll have a meeting at
Luc's in two weeks' time, said Marianne, the project's
leading lady. Luc said, 'Don't be ridiculous, it'll never
work. Stick to writing. At least you won't run up any
bills.'

The day of the meeting I was making curtains and
realized I had forgotten to do anything about the
recipe. At lunchtime, just before the two-o'clock
kitchen meeting, I let myself into Luc's surgery while
he was out at the pizzeria, dialled up 'cherry pie' on
the Internet, and was able, within seconds, to down-
load a short-crust-pastry recipe from a source in
Tennessee. I had a problem with the printer, which
recognized I was English and kept trying to form a
queue. When Luc printed out a prescription and insurance form for his first patient after lunch, the
computer started producing a neat set of instructions
which began, 'Pick 'em ripe and juicy.'

Luc was right, the cherry-pie project did not seem set

to be a winner. Even if you have sixty cherry trees that ripen on the hillside every April, it's a long way from that to a cherry pie. You need to spray them for blight – organic spray made from nettles, so you need some nettle beds, too – you need ladders and a workforce to pick them; de-stoning volunteers; huge pans to simmer them in; sugar; ovens; pastry bowls; large quantities of flour and butter; baking dishes; freezers; licences to cook and to sell, and something to do for an income the other eleven months of the year.

Even so, I told Marianne she should go and see someone called Bruno, who was on the town council. He was popular with everyone. He had a nice face and was funny and inquisitive. His wife, though Catalan, had a touch of the shires about her and drove around in a Range-Rover with her ash-blond hair in a ponytail. Bruno would give Marianne advice about the laws covering preparation of food for commercial use. 'The fat bastard who drives a city jeep?' she said.

Marianne, who seemed to have been torched into feminism by a neglectful husband, had run away down here from Paris with three children, bought a horse and a patch of land with sixty cherry trees on it and lived in a constant state of incipient outrage against the state, the mayor, men, marriage and, apparently, her own children. 'No-one on the town council's going to get involved with a hare-brained scheme like this right now,' she said. 'Not with the election coming up.'

By the time the election was over Marianne seemed to have decided to let the project slide. At the first meeting of the new town council, they were about to take a vote on whether they could make Subleyras stump up for the cancelled Johnny Hallyday concert. Bruno was doodling on his minutes when the door opened and one of the secretaries came in and quietly handed him a piece of paper. The vote was a resounding yes, though everybody knew it was probably unenforceable. Bruno opened his note. It was from Marianne. He knew who she was because the previous week she had come to consult him about the restrictions applying to the commercial preparation of food in a private kitchen, or in someone's dairy. The note gave the name of one of the town's luxury hotels: '*Chambre neuf, huit heures.*' He tried to recall her face. It was seven thirty. The mayor was asking whether anyone had any other business. Half an hour later he walked into *chambre neuf* to find Marianne lounging on the bed with a bottle of champagne on ice, Laurent Perrier rosé, beside her and, at the desk on his way out, a Visa slip waiting to be signed. When Stefan heard about this he said, 'It's a shame she's not pretty; I could almost fancy her myself.'

TV Special

A television crew arrived from Paris to film a live broadcast from the museum for a weekly show that went out at midnight. Because Luc's paintings were still up in the main exhibition space, Barbara, the *directrice*, asked him to appear. The other guests were the painter who had painted *Woman Met in Martinique, Who Left Me*, a local wine producer and Luc's friend, the poet and musician Pablo Baroja, together with his band.

Pablo's face was always twisted with worry, as though he had a stomach ulcer or was about to miss a train. He wore a frock coat and top hat, and all the band members had that look of the really fashionable people at university, the ones who say little, shave less and are incredibly skinny, despite the fact that they eat fry-ups and chip butties and drink spirits straight from the bottle. Their music was based on Catalan folk and dance tunes. Their instruments were all somehow hokey cokey – pipes that wheezed, tiny quarter-sized pianos with strings missing, a home-made violin. They made a noise like a scratch street ensemble, and yet the overall effect was surprisingly sonorous. Luc called it 'Oops, I almost made music music', and it suited his feeling that beauty was always the product of a mistake.

The whole thing was only just this side of a circus.

The presenter was completely distracted by a woman in the audience, Carla, who had recently married a nice English boy with a public-school background, who had put her through 'Dear Lord and Father of Mankind' and 'Jerusalem' at the wedding and had allegedly beaten her up in a last-ditch attempt to mend her foolish ways on the honeymoon. She was quite unaware of the presenter's agitation, and sat there winding her hair round her finger and admiring her shoes. I saw all this live as it went out on TV, because Luc hadn't wanted me to attend the show in case it put him off. Duncan had come down to my flat with his video recorder so I could make a tape to send to my parents. The moment Luc opened his mouth, the tape flew out of the slot and slithered off across the floor. 'My God!' Duncan shouted. 'Catch it. Quick! Stuff it in again.' We missed the whole of Luc's interview and had to explain later that a technical fault of an unforeseeable nature had come between Luc and his presentation on film to his future possible parents-in-law. The credits rose over a shot of an unlikely combination of people – Gigi and Catherine, with Stefan between them – bobbing up and down with their hands high in the air, performing the sardane, the Catalan dance, outside the museum entrance, even though it was by now one o'clock in the morning. I found Luc leaning against the wall of the museum, clutching the white clockwork rabbit who played percussion in Pablo's band. The TV presenter was trying to persuade Carla to come back to his hotel for a drink even as she climbed onto the back of another man's motorbike. Stefan caught me in the street and said, 'Were you there? Did you hear what he said? Did you hear what Luc said? He's such an arrogant shit.'

'No, I didn't,' I said, 'but here he is, why don't you tell him yourself.'

I explained about the broken tape.

'Never mind,' Luc said. 'All this, it's only tourist rubbish.' Later, when we were alone, he said, 'That was a bit of a coincidence, wasn't it, the business with the tape? It must have just been a coincidence.'

'A coincidence of what?'

'That it breaks, and just when you need it.'

'It's not going to break any other time,' I said. 'Not when it's just sitting in a cupboard. There's no point making an issue of it. That sort of thing happens all the time.'

'Not to me, it doesn't,' he said. 'It may do to you,' though of course it didn't, and I'd only said it to make him feel better. His mother had made a tape anyway.

'Can I send that to my parents then? Can't we make a copy?'

'Forget it,' he said. 'These things happen for a reason. It's too late now. Just don't bring it up again.'

Stefan 2

Stefan and Colette, his partner, were open with each other about their respective liaisons and often discussed them in front of their teenage daughter, who found her parents hopelessly naïve, politically and sentimentally. When the *lycéens* went on strike for longer or shorter hours, or better teaching, Heloïse was the only pupil in the entire school who refused to go on strike. As Gide says, when fish die they rise to the surface, belly up; it's their way of falling. In that respect she was not a disappointment to her parents. When she was a tiny child, Stefan used to take her to see violent films at the cinema during the afternoon, thinking she would grow up inured to violence and able to face the world without the slightest fear. Instead she had to be carried screaming from the cinema every time. Even now that she's grown-up she runs out the minute someone unsheathes a knife.

When they first arrived in the village, Colette was busy setting up her osteopathy practice and was usually late home at night and tired. Stefan would have spent the day walking in the hills with his daughter on his back, or converting the four stone walls they had bought, which had once been the tripe shop, and still had the word '*Triperie*' painted on the outside. Now it's like a ship inside. Everything is either glass, steel or wood. There is no furniture; everything was built-in to fit the house. Stefan says when you move on you should take nothing with you. He must be infuriating to live with. He had so much repressed revolutionary energy that when Colette returned in the evening he was always bursting to go out, while she wanted an early night.

Shortly after they moved in they were invited out to dinner at one of the modern houses on the hill just beyond the village, where the bourgeoisie had room for their swimming pools and outside dining areas and saunas. The host was an academic at the local university. His wife had been his research assistant, had raised their two children and was now lounging around, looking after her body and preparing dinners.

Stefan went alone and found himself sitting next to the hostess. The other guests were all people with money and jobs. He decided he must have been invited along because of his supposed intellectual credentials.

All the women were dressed extremely provocatively, he said, and the conversation was full of double entendres and references to group sex. He found it all rather overwhelming, although he never could resist a sexy bourgeoise rubbing her knee against his under the table. Sensing the mood of the evening, he told a story about his friend Noel, who worked selling fruit down the telephone lines from an international market in Perpignan. A woman he spoke to daily, but whom he had never met, rang him one morning and asked him to meet her the following day in a hotel on the road to Narbonne. She was a buyer for a supermarket chain in Marseilles. She gave him the address of the hotel, a motorway inn, with entrance codes and no bars or service, just vending machines. He drove to the rendezvous with an open mind, and found the fruit buyer in a completely darkened room, in bed, ready to receive him. He has never seen her face, but he knows her voice and touch and smell. They meet like this once a year, on her birthday. The rest of the year they speak on the phone, but never directly allude to what, for each of them, is a source of immense, grateful happiness.

Most of the guests left, more or less drunk, but when Stefan started to say goodnight, the host said no, they were enjoying his company far too much, it was time for another drink and then a dip.

The hostess led him out to the pool, which was sympathetically lit and warm, even though it was now past midnight. In the water, she wrapped herself around him and he thought, I'd rather do this somewhere dry. He pulled her out of the pool and began to lead her back into the sitting room. As they picked up their towels, he noticed the husband watching them from what was clearly their bedroom window, right above the pool. Each of them, in their different ways, he guessed, got something out of her humping the local revolutionary not-quite terrorist on the sofa bed after dinner and a refreshing plunge in the pool.

He lay on the sofa with his eyes clamped blissfully on the old-fashioned light fittings, which he said were curiously out of keeping with the contemporary decor, as though they had forgotten to update them. She was just about to set upon him when the husband stormed into the room with a camera and fired off a shot with a flash. The wife bucked her head up and shouted, 'Run!' Stefan fled into the garden, grabbed his clothes from by the edge of the pool and vaulted over the gate. Afterwards he said, shame-faced, I don't know why I did that. It was as though I had been programmed all evening to behave like a lover to an adulterous bourgeois hostess.

When he got home he woke Colette and told her the

whole story. He said, 'I feel very compromised by this running away thing. Why did I do it? It's against all my principles. I'd better go back and explain.'

Colette said, 'I should leave them to it for tonight. Maybe do something about it in the morning.'

Not long after Colette had left for work the following morning, Stefan received a call from the wife. She said her husband was out of his mind with rage. Stefan said he'd thought he was doing him a favour. You must be joking, she said. He's sending your wife a print of the photo. 'Oh good,' Stefan said, 'I was hoping we'd get a copy. Colette was curious to see your furniture; she's interested in that sort of thing because we don't have any at home.'

Later that day Stefan got a second call. This time it was the husband, asking him to meet up at the café. Stefan agreed, but on condition there was no embarrassing post-cuckold scene. The revolution may not have been an unqualified success, he said, there may be ground still to cover, but I think we can consider certain little victories were not in vain.

Over a beer, the husband said he had reconsidered the events of the previous evening. He was deeply sorry for any irritation or embarrassment, and he felt that Stefan had taught them something as a couple. Would he now kindly teach them a little more and do them the honour of joining them both that evening in their pool. And Stefan's wife, of course, as well, if she was in the mood. He felt that he and his wife had perhaps only paid lip service to the social developments of the previous ten to fifteen years, and it was time for them to consider some radical changes to their lifestyle. He also said that if Stefan had misread the situation the night before, it must have been because he and his wife were unconsciously willing something like that to happen.

'You don't say,' Stefan said. He didn't have much time for the unconscious.

'So what did you say?'

'For heaven's sake,' he said, 'I'm not some kind of rent boy. I'm not going to take a woman because her husband offers her to me for the good of her political education!'

'Oh,' I said, rather disappointed. 'So what did happen?'

'I screwed her behind his back,' he said. 'I've never been into group sex anyway. I know I should, but I just go limp whenever it comes up.'

He was always trying to drum into me that love affairs were dangerous because people who believed in love always thought they could make their own rules. In this respect, he said, Luc was lethal. You should always be suspicious of those who had no aspirations for society as a whole. There was no system to their seductions. There was safety in complexity; the people to watch were those who talked about simplicity and truth.

Marie-Lou

I wasn't the only girlfriend of an ex-lover that Gigi dressed. There was also Marie-Lou, who taught at the local dance school. Marie-Lou had been born in the village to a daft Spanish mother, who was all hairspray, tottery shoes and fake mantillas bought in the cheap tourist shops in Le Perthus, and a French father with an angry nose and a stoop, who'd been in the army and fought the Algerians. They moved to Nice when Marie-Lou was seven.

When Marie-Lou was fourteen, and almost as tall as she is now, she went with her mother to Aix-en-Provence for the day to buy material for a frock for her eldest brother's wedding. Her brother was a policeman who spent his time policing Algerians in particular, in the family tradition. Marie-Lou's legs started at her mother's shoulders. She wore a tiny boob tube, wrapped round her breasts like a fan belt. Her mother had lashings of black hair that was swept up on the top of her head. As Marie-Lou grew, her mother dressed her hair higher, to keep just ahead of her daughter. The mother had been up all night trying to calculate how much material she'd need for the two dresses – Marie-Lou's and her sister's – and whether anyone would notice if she cut Marie-Lou's on the nap and her sister's across it. 'I think we can get away with it,' she was saying, when she realized that Marie-Lou was no longer there. She turned and looked back down the street.

Marie-Lou was standing gracelessly, stranded on the pavement with her feet splayed, stomach muscles slack, mouth wide open, and her hands knotted and pressing into the small of her beautifully curved back. A man sitting at a café table thirty yards away had risen to his feet. A Moroccan street musician was playing something between a shawm and an oboe, doodling hypnotically with the end of it in the hot noon air. The man, a Turk, came towards Marie-Lou and held out his hand to her.

They danced to the music of the Moroccan shawm player till the streets had emptied. Siesta time. Marie-Lou's mother was asleep at the café table under the awning. The Turkish dancer took Marie-Lou up to his room in the hotel above the café and released her new breasts from the elastic tube. She wriggled out of her cotton trousers and they danced some more. The bed creaked plaintively in the afternoon silence as they consumed, erupted and then lay trembling, still.

The man turned out to be a great teacher. He was from Istanbul; he had once run the dance conservatoire there. He had a wife, and together they now ran an academy in Aix-en-Provence. Marie-Lou had been dancing since she was four. Lately she'd been thinking of giving it up because she only ever seemed to get taller. But the Turkish man liked that; he told her she must keep on growing, up and up. She should have no fear of anything; she could be as big as she liked. Let no ceiling stand in her way.

So Marie-Lou danced and grew, and the mother went home to Nice and said Marie-Lou would be back in a few years' time. She lived with the man and his wife, and danced for both of them. She says they were like parents to her, except it was better than that because she got to sleep with them, too. Then one day, two years later, she met another man in a bar who sold carpets and took her home to his attic room, and she danced a carpet dance for him, which involved her getting wrapped up in a rug. She stayed with him for a week, then went back home to her Turkish parents, arriving one morning with a half-eaten almond croissant in a paper bag and throwing up on the staircase.

Her real parents had moved back to the village to be near the other daughter and her husband, a car mechanic at the garage by the Devil's Bridge. When Amelia, Marie-Lou's daughter, was born, Marie-Lou's mother, a Le Penist by temperament and conviction, felt a powerful love for the dark-skinned, black-eyed baby such as she had never felt for her own children, and she adopted her as her own. Marie-Lou was too young to cope, and she still had her career as a dancer to pursue. Amelia slept in her grandmother's bed until she was nine years old. She was one of those grand-mothers it was easy to imagine in bed, with her hair down her back and a nightdress that suggested she had not entirely renounced all sexual aspiration. Luc said her husband would lie like a wolf across the threshold, in his daytime clothing, through the night. Then Marie-Lou's knees cracked and she came home to have them operated on. At that point she met Christophe.

Christophe was in his fifties. He had been born in Lyon, and his mother had left him with his father when he was two. Her name was never mentioned again, up to the moment his father died, two years earlier. Then Marie-Lou looked up all the people in France with Christophe's family name, did some research at the births, marriages and deaths office in Paris, and came up with a list of one, a woman living in Lyon. One night she wrote the number down for Christophe. Ring when you're ready, she told him and went off to erect the scenery for the next night's performance of *Pierrot et Columbine*. Christophe drank two whiskies and picked up the phone. A woman's voice, old and frail and frightened, answered. He told her his name. She hung up. Since then he hasn't tried again. But he and Marie-Lou have in common the feeling that they don't quite belong to their parents.

Christophe studied theatre and politics, so when 1968 came around he was well placed. He'd married an actress, a great beauty who had had small parts in Godard films, and was as strong as Moreau, as voluptuous as Bardot. She was a radical, too. When the revolution was over, Christophe trained to be a French teacher and was posted to the village. His wife, who was expecting their second child, came too. She was never happy there. While Christophe relished the life of a small town, adored by his pupils – among them Luc – politicizing them, leading them on demonstrations to the *mairie* to demand longer playtimes, or encouraging them to burn their copies of Racine, his wife sat at home with the babies and grew heavy with fear of growing old and nothing ever happening again. When the children were in their late teens, she took their car and a bottle of bourbon up the mountain, and set off back down with the manic bravado of an unskilled skier on a black run. The car ploughed up seven trees before coming to a terrible, silent standstill in the cork forest, with seven hairpin bends still to go.

At first Christophe went crazy. He slept with his pupils and took to drink. They had just had plans drawn up for a new house, to be constructed in fields by the river, five minutes' drive from the town. It was a part of the valley that was unusually blessed, and where plants grow thick and waxy and there are flowers all year round. It was to be a house for his wife, where she might start to be happy again.

Christophe was going to cancel the project, but Luc persuaded him to go ahead with it. You have to continue; you have to build a house for someone to come and live in. You can't keep on sleeping in women's beds and leaving in the morning all your life. So the house was built, and Marie-Lou arrived.

There was an age difference of twenty-eight years between them. Christophe was short and stocky – he cut down his drinking when he met Marie-Lou, so his face lost a lot of fat, but not the flesh to contain it, which gave him a deflated look. He had an incredibly deep voice, big forearms and a graceful walk. Marie-Lou was a clown, twice his height, always throwing her arms around him and kissing him, gasping and shrieking at her own mistakes. She called him '*mon amour*'. Together they put on end-of-year shows for Marie-Lou's dance school at the Salle de Spectacle. Christophe introduced her to his record collection. You got the impression they spent a lot of time in bed. Marie-Lou's parents hated Christophe because he was a communist, and refused to let him meet Amelia. Marie-Lou saw her daughter just once a week, in the front line of her ballet class.

One night, during a village fête, we were all sitting at the Central drinking. Marie-Lou screeched, leaped to her feet and dragged me across the square to where a young man from the local rugby team was dancing naked on a table. After a while we came back. I hadn't found it very exciting, nor had Marie-Lou; it was just in her nature to goggle and applaud and notice the world going on around her. Later, I noticed Christophe hadn't spoken to her for an hour. She went to a stall opposite the café and bought a huge bag of sweets, disappeared behind the Roman wall and ate them all in

149

one go. Then she dived into the Central, and came out again ten minutes later smelling of sugar and sick. They went home. Two days later I met her wearing a hat in the street. It was July, so I asked her why she was wearing a woollen hat. She took it off and showed me where she had ripped out all the hair from the crown of her head that night when they'd got home, because Christophe had said he wasn't prepared to live with a woman who catcalled at naked men. He'd said it would make people think he was too old to get it up.

We often ate at the pizzeria in summer. Marie-Lou would order three pizzas – plain margheritas, with tomato, cheese and a thin base – and eat one after the other. If anyone had a dessert she would say, 'I'll have another pizza please.' She burned it all off dancing, and probably in bed with Christophe. She was always angling for the last glass out of the bottle of wine whenever we went to a restaurant, so that she could declare, according to custom, that she would marry within the year. But Christophe didn't want to marry her. He couldn't imagine them married, though they'd been living together, in the house he'd built for his wife, for six or seven years. He said if he married again he would turn into an old man overnight.

Gigi had been one of Christophe's lovers for a short time. One day Annie, the chemist's wife, and Gigi were shopping in Perpignan together. Gigi was about to say to her, 'Listen, you'll never guess, I slept with Christophe last night!' when Annie got in first and said, 'I'm so in love with Christophe, I can't eat.' So instead Gigi said, 'Oh, you can't fancy him; he's far too old.'

Gigi didn't approve of Marie-Lou because she said she was stupid and had no grace, despite being a dancer. She was powerful and astonishing, but she had no grace. Nothing in Gigi's shop fitted her. But on a

Saturday morning, while Christophe was raking through the CD stall at the market, Gigi beckoned Marie-Lou inside. Just stand there, she said, and slip this dress on. It was a wedding dress by Ines de la Fressange. I came into the shop to pay for a skirt I'd taken the week before. Gigi was always happy to give credit if you agreed to wear the piece of clothing all the time so that others would come and buy the same. Marie-Lou looked extraordinary in the dress. She turned round, and there was Christophe looking at her through the window. Gigi smiled her wide, pale smile, and shrugged and went out to talk to him, leaving Marie-Lou feeling stupid in the dress. Gigi was so seductive it was absurd; she made insincerity captivating, and yet she was terribly fond of Christophe, and of Luc, too, so it wasn't real, only fake insincerity. She took Christophe off for a coffee over the road, and Marie-Lou and I went off to the market to buy things for lunch.

I then went back to the café to wait for the others. Christophe had bought sliced *saucisse de montagne* for us to eat out of waxed paper with our aperitifs. He was telling Luc about the wedding dress. 'I can't do it,' he said. 'I don't want to marry her. I can't be faithful. I have been so far, but what if I met another woman?' At that point he flicked his head round, afraid Marie-Lou might have come up behind and overheard him. We saw his eyes fix on a woman in a red shirt, making her way up towards the top of the market. He said, 'Wait there, I'll be back.'

He followed the woman up past Etienne's spice stall, and the trout van, where a man in a white coat whacked each fish over the head to order. The crowd was thinning out as it was past midday, but Christophe had difficulty keeping up with the woman.

'I had to talk to her,' he said later. 'I felt her pass. I had to follow her. I thought it was her.'

'Who?'

'I don't know. The woman I was meant to . . . I can't remember. I just had to speak to her. It was the woman I was talking about. I tapped her on the shoulder; she turned round.'

'And?' we both said.

'It was me,' said Marie-Lou.

The Beach

If you live near the sea, you have to go there every now and then. At some time people must have started wandering down to the sea's edge just because they wanted to be close to it, not because they were setting sail or hoping to catch fish. Is it because we came out of the sea in the first place, at the start of evolution, that we now feel pulled back to look at it, be close to it, play, flirt or read our newspapers alongside it?

The English, in particular, feel comfortable by the sea. Not that our sea does much for us; it's cold, unapproachable and cement grey most of the time. There was no way I was ever going to live near the Atlantic. But having the Mediterranean so close was very different from knowing you were only forty-five miles from Skegness, the face of the sea in my childhood. In the summer holidays the family would go for outings to confront the sea, as though it was us v Poseidon and the tideline was a net. The sea would always win, either retreating so far off behind the base line you simply couldn't engage with it, or zooming in and flooding your patch of ground, sending you scarpering back up to the car park. The Mediterranean is round. That makes a difference to the way you feel about it: there is no confrontational shore.

The village is only thirty kilometres from the sea,

and there is only one beach anyone goes to. There are other, nearer beaches, and there are hidden coves once you get over into Spain, but this is the backyard beach, a little bit of the village by the sea, where you can always find room to sit and meet people you know.

A straight Roman road runs from the village to the sea. As you approach you can see another Templar castle at Collioure, set up high on the cliff. Like the one further up the coast, it was never used. The French have always been strong on the unactivated deterrent.

Cut into the cliff is a monument to Walter Benjamin, the Jewish scholar from Berlin. This was not where he should have died. In wartime people die in places they were never supposed to, in places meant to be a passageway, not a resting place. It's like dying halfway up the stairs or in the shed. Commissioned to construct a monument for the centenary of Benjamin's birth, the architect constructed a rectangular iron shaft, maybe two metres high, two metres wide and 200 steps deep, and laid it not vertically, but at an angle to the cliff, like a staircase. If you stand at the top of the cliff, looking down the funnel with the light behind you, your reflection is thrown down onto a glass sheet, fixed just short of the surface of the sea. You see your own body, prostrate, as it would hit the water if you fell.

No-one knows where Benjamin's body lies or where his bones might be. He disappeared in 1940 after a three-day hike across the border shrubland. Thirsty, unfit for further travel and bewildered by the place of refuge, which often provokes a violent nostalgia for the dangerous place one has been forced to leave, he slept a night in a guest house in Banyuls. It's said that the woman who ran the guest house where he slept denounced him to the Germans, who killed him. He was a bespectacled, academic man, one of those timid, unexpected wartime heroes whose bravery is of the kind acknowledged only in peacetime. It would have been easier to kill Benjamin than a fly, and then flick the body away into the sea.

Just north of here the new fast road starts to climb and you are lifted to a point where the sea is below you, dark blue and surprisingly deep, with little white scratches where a boat has passed, and pink and yellow and green and red dashes of sail, like cotton cuffs peeking from a sombre suit. The soil in the vineyards on the terraced cliffs is brick red, and the vines produce a grape which is made into a thick, black glutinous wine, to drink with the *poivrons aux anchois*, red peppers and anchovies, powdered with silver leaf and packed in crushed flakes of sea salt – Collioure's local dish. Collioure is where Matisse made his home. Its distinguishing feature is the phallic bell tower on the end of the harbour promontory, a flesh pink knob winking rosily.

It's the last long beach in France before the coast crumples into coves and creeks, like a wrinkled elbow joint. At one end it is still a smooth, long, sandy expanse, and at the other it is already beginning to crinkle and grow rocky. Once you are safely into Spain, and round the treacherous headland of Cap Creus, where Salvador Dali built his house, the coastline smooths out once again.

Leave the main road here and follow the smaller one under the coast road, through a tunnel and up onto the track that goes down to the beach village. Until quite recently it was no more than three lines of houses, maybe fifteen in each, built on the beach in the 1930s to house Spanish refugees and later 'enemy aliens' interned by the French during the early stages of the war. The refugees built them, watched over by the French army, who didn't know whether they should put locks on the inside or outside of the doors.

The beach houses are simple, usually one-storey buildings, with sand tracks running between them. They were sold off just after the war, and the locals snapped them up, and planted bougainvillea and passion flowers up trellises nailed into the concrete walls, and created little gardens of pebbles and cacti and sea plants that thrive in salt. Sometimes we spent the night in Luc's family's house, in a large, sandy upper room twenty yards from the edge of the sea. Downstairs all the furniture came from Luc's grandmother's house – dark mahogany dressers and a solid table covered with a washable plastic cloth, with twisted legs, wrung out like a bathing costume to remove the salt water. Upstairs the front wall is all glass. Lying in bed you see only three elements – sky, sea and, in the morning, the rising sun.

The family spent their summers at the beach, where they had a house which had originally been constructed to house German internees – mostly Jewish, before the French decided whose side they were on – and Spanish refugees. The boys had a boat, which they sailed in competitions. Their grandmother occasionally guarded them at the beach when they were very small. She would tie a long piece of black elastic round each of their waists, which allowed them to stray from the porch of the beach house to the edge of the water, no further. If they went into the water the elastic would snap and lash them across the buttocks or the backs of their legs.

Mothers and children spend most of the long summer holidays at the beach, while fathers stay back in the village and drive down at night to eat grilled fish after a swim or a surf and a game of volleyball with the children. The crowd starts gathering around ten in the morning. In early summer Catherine steals down to the beach when she has fed her horses and watered her garden. She brings a book and lies at first on her back, while the sun is still weak, then, as it gains strength, she turns onto her front, her breasts making small saucer dimples in the sand. Stefan sometimes comes down early, to swim, he says, before the wind-surfers and motor boats take to the water, but really he goes to see Catherine, enjoying the delicious early-morning tension in his loins, aroused, he says, by the sight of her pubic hair spilling from the tight band of her bikini bottoms, like coils of sand worms on a damp beach.

At mid-morning the ice-cream sellers arrive – usually actors, or young men who went to circus school, as the children of many liberal bourgeois families seem to do. They weave their way through the crowd, black from the sun, with poodle curls or shaven heads and long flapping shorts to protect the backs of their thighs, the dye from the cloth washed away by June or early July, a whisper of the original colour. They sell Magnums and Cornettos, lollipops and fruit, which they carry in huge thermally sealed hampers, releasing quick gull-like cries as they weave up and down the beach, singing songs that have no sense but are to do with what they have in their hampers, and must be invitations to buy. If you stop them they will crouch down beside you and flick through the book you are reading and have put to one side to scrabble among the sun oil, tissues and sandals in your bag to find change. They are never ill-humoured or tired. Their teeth flash whiter than ice and they walk in the hot sand without wincing. They are strangely eunuch-like, and never seem to glance at the girls, or even the tumescent males, sprawled sleepily next to women with Botticelli breasts, enjoying the luxury of not noticing what they know is theirs to touch.

There is a sour delicacy to the etiquette of topless

bathing. You often see couples smiling lazily at one another; it is almost as though the social restriction imposed by the supposed anti-erotic aspect of naturism is welcome, since it no longer exists anywhere else, and brings a transgressional note to the slightest contact, even between couples who know each other's bodies of old.

The beach is a democratic place, and although there are surprises there is no judgement. It is a public place, and there is even a feeling of citizenship among the beachgoers, and of equality. Luc told me that one summer a group of friends came from the village for a holiday picnic, most of them in their mid-thirties or forties – the dress circle and all their husbands and boyfriends; in many cases both at once. Luc said that the chemist's wife arrived late. In the street she looks like a slightly dumpy mum, with a pleasant face and sensibly cut brown hair. When she pulled off her dress to go and swim, the others all watched her walk towards the water. Without her clothes on she was a series of swoops and curves and lovely flesh, and as she stood with the sea just up to the very tops of her legs, tickling the crease between her thighs and her buttocks, with her back to them all, in her plain brown halter-neck swimsuit, adjusting the tie at the back of her neck, they all just lay looking after her, speechless. Shortly afterwards her husband, the chemist with the extra spring, got up and followed her into the water.

Grandparents encourage toddlers to walk on the soft sand, to give them an easy landing, which isn't very good training for life, but makes falling down fun. Clusters of adolescents arrange themselves on the sand, boys and girls mixed, the dark and the fair, the gangly and tubby and bookish and the astonishingly beautiful, legs like compasses, dancing circles in the sand, with their black hair licked back by the waves and dusty with dried salt, skin glowing darkly like unglazed terracotta steeped in some aromatic oil. Now and then a boy leaps to his feet in anger and runs off, very fast, down the beach, and a girl shrugs and turns back to her friends. He will slouch back later and fling himself onto the sand with his back to her, and she will continue to laugh and chatter with all the hardened know-how of a woman twice her age. Younger children are busy building things, carrying bits of the beach over to where they are making a rival beach, or a city or a fortress, copying the world as they know it. Mothers stand around in halter-tops and sarongs, holding the youngest child in their arms, the last child, the one made for sheer pleasure, as a keepsake, almost, of a time in their lives that is passing with the oldest child's application to university or first trip to England to be an au pair. After supper the older couples, whose children are elsewhere, or off at a village ball, stroll along the shore and stop to talk with friends, much as they do at home. It seems a nice way to spend your life, ebbing and flowing like the tide between the village and the shore. Up to 15 August the sky is a hot metal press, the sea an unmarked surface. On the night of the fifteenth there are almost always green comets and shooting stars in the sky, and phosphorescence in the sea and fireflies in the air. Then there are two weeks of variable weather; it may carry on as before, but once the fifteenth has passed this is a favour, not a right. It may grow stormy, as though the season had suddenly become adult, tired of games and sunshine, and had brought on some heavy weather to call the idle to order. In September, when the children go back to school, people pack up and go back inland, and shore up and shutter their beach houses against the equinox storms with metal blinds, padlocked to stanchions set in concrete in the ground.

Each year a house is lost, or partially wrecked by the sea, which rises spookily from its summer slumber to fling itself in a lunatic rage against the land. It is as though, courted all summer long, played with, loved, embraced and serenaded, the sea had woken to find itself abandoned and come to throw itself at the coast line with all the mad gestures of a locked-out lover.

The beach is at its best, is most itself, in the grey, scowling afternoons of early autumn, when the wind has blown great troughs into the beach, and the sand is already piled up high against the house walls, and grit has pelted and scratched the metal sheaths, pinging and rattling, a percussion of minerals wielded by the wind. There is always a shoe and a toy, and the odd unidentifiable strut or piece of piping from a wind-surfer or a barbecue grill, and a fish head dried to a husk in the corner between sill and window. Now you can walk across the rocks and into the next bay, where the vegetation is terse and acrid – garden rosemary's salty cousin, grey with the weather and the sun and wind, with tiny pinches of lilac-blue flowers in the winter. There is a sea shrub with pink flowers edged with yellow, and sea artichokes, huge donkey thistles with stems as coarse as sugar cane, which ooze white, bubbling sap when they snap and break.

UFO

'*Tu m'aimes?*'

'No. Only *amoureuse*,' I tell him, though I don't know if it's true.

When Luc touches my face his fingers are bone dry and professional. It's reassuring. He is not a reassuring person, but his fingers are, accustomed to the intricate scale of the tooth.

It was always a surprise to wake up there. It felt like somewhere you woke up and had to guess where you were, as though you'd been transported in a sack, like a cat, or washed up on a shore while you slept.

Luc said it was normal. He was always saying '*C'est normal*,' though hardly anything was. 'You've come from another planet. *Bienvenue.*'

'Your time here', he explained in a pleasant, easy-listening voice, as though I were a visitor being shown round a factory in a hard hat, 'is probably only equivalent to a single day in your own world. You'll get back to the place you can't remember for now, and find nothing has changed. There'll still be a half-drunk cup of coffee on the kitchen table and a sheet of paper in your typewriter.

'You've forgotten, for now, because you're new here and *amoureuse*. But as the years go by, and your children grow, and you watch me every day, doing the same things, growing a bit older, a little bit will come back every day, just a tiny bit of the picture. One day,' he said, lying down beside me again, his eyes closed, touching my cheek, his voice so close to my ear that his lips brushed against it, 'I'll be down in the barn, painting, I'll hear a crash of plates and a cry and I'll think *Oh merde, ça y est. C'est fini. Elle va partir*. When I get upstairs I'll just find the broken crockery and a few grey hairs in your hairbrush. There'll be a humming noise, and I'll go down and find the grass all singed down the end of the field and a dark round shape disappearing over the mountain.' He liked the idea of UFOs.

'It'll just be there, waiting?'

'It's always there.'

He pointed to where the field dipped away and the dark seam of the wood blurred in the emptying light of dusk. 'Look, it's there now. Are you telling me you can't see it?'

I closed my eyes. 'I can't.'

'Good,' he said. 'I'm glad to hear it.'

He got off the bed and whistled to the dog. I got used to his changes of speed after a bit. Very reasonably, *sur un ton raisonnable*, as though to the dog, who didn't care anyway, he added, 'I hope it stays that way.'

We rarely left the village. Once we met a man who lived a kilometre from the town centre. I asked Luc if he lived far away. 'Oh yes,' he said. 'After the Pont du Diable.'

I kept myself happy writing for six hours a day, then cooking, riding and gardening, or watching him paint. Occasionally I'd think, This is not my life. It's wonderful, but it's not my life. But then I tried to think what I'd be doing otherwise. I imagined being back in England, the place I'd left, sitting in wine bars, or sailing up escalators, reading the adverts for holidays and books, or looking for parking places, or temping somewhere and buying salad leaves ready washed from Marks & Spencer, or doing a teacher-training course, and none of that seemed very possible, either. All those things were as prefabricated and pre-packaged as the salad leaves. I wanted to feel I was making up my own story. I was making up a story, *mon histoire*, but it wasn't actually mine.

Most people said he was crazy, a dreamer whose mother had cuddled him too long and who had turned out a weird mix of gentle idealist and vigorous monk – the kind who lugged stones or felled trees. He was also a fantastic gossip, which I loved, and when I wonder now how we spent all those winter nights, it must have been mostly swapping stories by the fire, trying to tell each other our lives, to see if it made any difference to anything. We were completely antisocial, though Luc knew everyone. I was introduced to all the locals, the newspaper editor, the people he'd been to school with, the man who owned all the cork forests, the painters and poets and cowboys, and Gigi and her friends, and his parents and all their friends, and the people who ran the restaurants and their girlfriends, and the famous poet from Paris, so famous that Paul Auster did his university thesis on him and Luc had gone out with his daughter.

We sometimes had dinner with the elderly poet and his wife when they came down from Paris for July and August. She was fair and spoke as though she were auditioning for the part of Cordelia in *King Lear*, constantly true and somehow pure and tender, in a way that got on my nerves. She also insisted on refer-ring to her daughter in every other sentence, which I wouldn't have minded, except she had the same name as me, so it had the curious effect of neutralizing my presence, as though she had reinvented the foursome, and in fact her daughter was really in my place and I was an extra they'd rung up to walk the part at the last minute.

Women, generally speaking, were tricky. There was Marie-Lou, and there was Gigi, and Angélique with her sandwich bar, and Barbara with the museum, but apart from them none of the women actually seemed to have any public life at all, apart from in the shops. They were far too busy with their children's lives, and they were suspicious of a woman who had no children and wrote books that weren't on sale in their bookshop. I soon learned to dress appropriately – no more shorts or ripped jeans – but I still looked slightly hippyish to them because I occasionally dressed in the casual way English people do. The men were all nice to me in the cafés, and people like Henri showed me their porno-graphic texts, displaying their vulnerable spots with a candour and trust I found appealing, though Luc insisted on reading them all through first. Luc was worried that there wasn't enough for me to do. He found it surprising that I preferred talking to my girlfriends in England on the telephone to making new friends in the village. He decided we should buy a piano.

Piano 1

We found one in Paris, in a huge music shop in the Rue de Rennes. They sold sheet music on the ground floor, woodwind on the second, strings on the third, uprights on the fourth and grand pianos on the fifth. They obviously liked to make things difficult for themselves. We'd been to buy Luc some riding boots. He was standing in the middle of the pavement in the Rue de Rennes in his faded blue denim shirt and jeans and a worn-out brown suede jacket, clutching his posh shoe-box, trying to persuade me to go inside and buy a piano.

I said, 'It won't fit in my flat.'

He said, 'We'll have it at the farm.'

It was odd, with all the traffic zooming past and the sun glinting off the Tour Montparnasse and him standing there with his riding boots, to think of a grand piano belonging to me in his house. It felt like a marriage proposal. I'd always thought a piano was for life. In the big house I'd shared with my ex-husband there had been two big black ones, placed nose to nose, like well-cared-for Labradors who think they're better than the servants. Long after we'd finished speaking we'd continued to play together, glancing at each other's reflections in the raised lids, nodding and catching each other's eye. I didn't mind that I'd never see them again, but they now seemed like symbols of bad luck.

What I really wanted, my dream piano, was something beaten up and sore, but with a beautiful tone. Just a simple upright, donated by a kind old person who had recognized, sadly, that her daughter's visits had petered out, that it was a long way for her to come from the Auvergne, that she scarcely touched it these days, the grandchildren had an electronic keyboard.

But by the end of that excruciating day, Luc and I were co-owners of a large, black lacquered Korean monster. I was intimidated by the saleswoman, who followed me around and, every time I moved on to a new piano, slid onto the stool of the one I'd just left and played the minute waltz by Chopin in forty-three seconds flat. I just wanted to get out of there fast. It seemed OK, and Luc put down the deposit. He always paid cash when we went out of town, as though he didn't believe his cheques could work if the person he was making it out to didn't know him, but here they had said they preferred a cheque. He didn't have a credit card. Whenever I paid for anything for us both, like dinner, with mine, he'd say, 'No, don't, I've got cash,' and if I insisted he would look away as I signed, as though he was unhappy about being party to anything dubious and was only turning a blind eye to keep me happy.

They would deliver the piano the following week, free of charge. We explained he lived after fifteen steep bends up a mountain, but they said they'd seen it, done it, all before. After we'd signed the papers we went and had a drink in a bar by the Hôtel de Ville on our way to have dinner with Luc's gallery owners, and we left all the piano documents on the counter. I always felt jumpy when we went to grand dinners, because Luc was capable of getting out his peasant's knife to hack at some bread or spear a chunk of cheese. The first time I saw him do it, it had reminded me of Emma Bovary's wedding night, when the servant brings in the food and Charles gets out his knife and Emma thinks, I've married a peasant. Halfway through dinner I realized I'd left the papers in the bar and ran back to fetch them. It took me so long to find the bar again that by the time I got back to the restaurant Luc and his two friends were walking their black poodle round the Place des Vosges for the fourth time. We went off and celebrated the recovery of the papers with a cognac in a café on the Rue Saint Antoine, during which the black poodle had an epileptic fit.

The next morning I said, 'Luc, I don't really want this piano. Let's just put an ad in the local newspaper, and get an old scruffy one. Let's go back to the shop now and tell them.'

Luc was trying on his new riding boots. We were staying in Marcel's flat. In the room next door, on the other side of a supposedly soundproof wall, we could hear the voice of a woman filling her analytic hour with flat words of woe. Luc said, 'It's too late. I gave them my word of honour.'

'No you didn't,' I said. 'You gave them a cheque.'

'Same thing,' he said. He really did believe that. I never saw him cheat anyone, never heard him tell even a white lie. He could use his brown gold eyes to get whatever he wanted; he was stubborn and proud, but never deceitful. It's good to be with a man who will never do anything that makes you feel ashamed for him, and who looks nice in a pair of boots. 'If you ever start seeing another man,' he once said, 'just tell me. Don't cheat, just let me know.' A child had been frightened one day in the dental chair, and while Luc's back was turned had leapt up and made for the door. Luc saw him and gently kicked the door shut. 'Sit down again,' he said, and the child did. 'Now. Do you want to leave?'

'Yes.'

'Why?'

'I don't know.'

'Are you frightened?'

'Yes.'

'OK then. Off you go.'

The day before the piano arrived I trapped a finger in the car door and had to show the removal men where to put it with my hand in a sling. Luc X-rayed it at the surgery, wrapped the image in a Kleenex and put it in his shoebox with his phone bills and income-tax demands, marked '*petit doigt*'.

He was at work when the piano arrived. The removal men slid it through the front door, which was a stable door, in two parts, so you could keep the bottom half closed and gaze moonily over the top half out into the field. They positioned it near the window and went out to smoke cigarettes under the lime tree. I signed for it and then they left. I sat and looked at it for a while. It looked more like the accessory of a dead person than a live one. It cried out for a bouquet of plastic chrysanthemums on the black lacquer lid to set off the crimson trimmings. The paint on the inside was exactly the shade of dull gold my brother had kept in a special little pot on his window ledge for touching up the details on his Airfix galleons.

Later that afternoon, Luc's father and mother walked over from the summer house to pay their respects to the piano. Their poodle came dancing in, skated over the wooden floor and sniffed its legs. Luc's mother sashayed over and struck a note with a scarlet fingernail, and leapt back laughing when it sounded, as though it were something ridiculous and newfangled. His father said it was good to have music again, that he hadn't heard any up here since Madame Desarthes played the 'Moonlight Sonata' in her black dress, with a glass of whisky on the edge of the piano. He had obviously forgotten Brigitte already – or she'd been airbrushed out – and didn't count Luc's habit of turning up the speakers full blast at sunset till the sound of Jimi Hendrix playing 'The Star-Spangled Banner' at Woodstock ricocheted off the southern flank of the Canigou. I didn't play because my hand was in the sling.

Luc and the dog got back in the early evening. The dog shuffled across as though they'd had a tiff, and threw herself down with a thud in the opposite corner on top of her pungent blanket. If she'd smoked it would have been the moment to light up. Luc looked startled to see how much space the piano took up in the room that had previously been so empty. It was a huge room, with a kitchen at one end, a fireplace, a shabby leather sofa, two odd chairs and a table from a convent, with little drawers at each place setting, where a nun might keep her wooden plate and her napkin, a missal and maybe something secret, too. Even Stefan loved the room. He said it had something you couldn't contrive, a real rustic quality, with every-thing slightly lopsided or the wrong shape.

Luc was brilliant at introducing false notes and then allowing them time to assimilate, for dust to settle on a plastic pen holder given to him by one of his patients, so that it didn't look out of place beside a tiny stone Buddha sitting comically in a niche, or the seat of a pair of jeans daubed with paint and pinned to the whitewashed wall, a token from a painter who had come for the weekend. But the piano could never have the air of having arrived by accident. It came in waving its embossed invitation, tricked out and ready to seduce. The far wall, from waist height to ceiling, was all glass. The mountain was set at the perfect distance, neither so close that it loomed heavily, nor so far that you didn't feel you could walk there in a day. Between the mas and the mountain the land rippled and dipped, and just outside the window the horses came and munched the new green walnuts off the tree. When the sun set, it poured over the floor like molten wax, and Luc would paint in his atelier below by the same light while I cooked or read upstairs. Now the sun hit the piano, and we had to cover it in its blanket, which made it look even more like a royal race horse than it did already. It was high summer – July – and there were flies everywhere because of the horses. Luc set out little dishes of vile yellow crystals to poison them, but they were out of date and you probably could have sprinkled them on your muesli with no ill effect. Somehow, though, the piano became a hospice for flies: it was where they went to die.

We tried to assimilate the beast. Friends and neighbours came to look at it, as they might have done if the bishop had brought a giraffe back with him from Africa. Two weeks later my finger was well enough for the splint to be removed. Alone in the house one day, I sat down at the piano. I had the music for the Schubert Impromptus that Brigitte had previously played. She'd taken her piano when she'd left. She and a girlfriend had hoisted it onto a trailer and towed it down the mountain. I started to play. There is something quite strange and solipsistic about making a noise in an empty house by playing a musical instrument. You find yourself clearing your throat awkwardly between movements, and shifting in your seat as though you were at the Festival Hall. I played all afternoon, with the flies dropping like flies into the heart of the piano, caught on the strings, flattened by the hammers, till the instrument seemed to be almost earning its keep as a flycatcher. The door opened, but it was always opening and shutting in the breeze, or as the dog slipped in and out, so I didn't take much notice. When I got up to fetch a glass of water, I realized Luc's uncle, who I hadn't seen since the Easter Sunday meal, was sitting in an armchair listening. Every year in early summer he went off up to his mas, a two-roomed stone house with table, a bed and a chair, where he drew all summer, returning at the end of September. He appeared to be dead. The glass in my hand slipped between my fingers and shattered on the stone floor by the sink. Even when you pass a dead rat, or a squirrel with its paws in the air, it seems to take a split second before you start inwardly, as the brain retorts to the eyes that this is not normal, that this thing should not be there.

He wasn't dead, though. He was watching me through half-closed eyes.

'Carry on,' he said, as though it were an audition, or one of those occasions when you had to play at a Sunday School concert for people who didn't care what you played, just as long as you weren't as advanced as their Ellie, who'd just got her grade five with merit. Afterwards he said I played quite well, but not as well as another girl he mentioned. When I asked Luc that evening who Eléonore was, he said she was the daughter of Uncle Jérôme's ex-mistress and that she didn't play the piano. But what surprised Luc was that Jérôme had been to the house at all that afternoon. Apparently he hadn't set foot in Luc's part of the farm for fifteen years. 'He heard about the piano,' Luc said. 'He came to see it while I wasn't here.' It worried him. It seemed like another dark sign.

Piano 2

Shortly afterwards we went up to Burgundy for an exhibition of Luc's paintings. For the first time he was sharing a show with his uncle, though Jérôme wasn't planning to attend. Luc's pictures were full of colour, and very simple and abstract. There was a family resemblance there – in the days when they had been close, Jérôme had taught him about modern art.

A couple of days before we left for Burgundy, a gallery owner from Marseilles called Jean-Marc Aurilly came to visit. Aurilly had been born in the village in the 1920s. He was frail and ashen, the son of a postman who had known Luc's grandmother well. He told stories about the war in the village, how they were made to produce food off the land which would be sent by rail back to Germany while they fed on rats and mice. I heard so many different versions of the war. Henri, for instance, said his mother had been a pretty wartime teenager in Montpellier, and had learned to dance in the arms of German soldiers, and still went misty-eyed whenever she heard Marlene Dietrich or recalled the feel of a leather collar against her cheek. I thought that would have made a better subject for a short story than the girls Henri met at the beach – his usual inspiration – but when I told him so he said indignantly, 'Hang on, I didn't say she *slept* with them.' Aurilly started out as a carpenter, but for some reason he left the village in the Fifties and set up a gallery of contemporary art in Marseilles. His gallery was very successful; he had a knack of spotting painters whom other gallery owners would later make famous. We went to the opening of a group exhibition, where he was showing a couple of Luc's paintings – mottled white with sepia strokes, like something found underneath when a fresco is peeled away from the wall. At the dinner for the painters afterwards, a man who had shown a cast-iron sculpture and had forearms like lorry tyres got into an argument with Luc about Uccello. Luc said he'd never heard of him and that he wasn't interested in the history of art. He knew perfectly well who Uccello was, but he hated artists talking about painting. He loved pretty much anything pre-1600 and post-1907. Anything in between was pompous crap. The sculptor wrote his phone number on a piece of rolled-up paper and slid it to me under the table. Underneath he'd written, 'When you get tired of this idiot ring me.'

Aurilly took his breakfast on the terrace outside the café at nine thirty, hoping someone he knew would pass, but the only person who ever did was me. He'd begun to suffer from moments of absence. The morning we left he had woken in his room in the hotel, panicked and rung his wife, about whom he was otherwise rather dismissive, and said, 'Where am I? Where am I? I don't know where I am.'

We drove up to Burgundy, leaving town in Luc's mother's tin car on a boiling-hot Thursday afternoon, and arriving after dark in a grey town on the river Seine. Luc hated it from the moment we arrived. I loved Burgundy, the churches, the vineyards, the abbeys, the mist – laid on a bit thick for July, but very atmospheric. The show was in a grey stone bourgeois house overlooking the river from a height. All the beau monde of Burgundy were there.

Luc was unhappy at that time because his life was about to change professionally. Until now he had only worked three days a week, spending the rest of the time painting and riding. Now his partner at the surgery was taking early retirement. His eldest daughter had killed herself only a few months before. At first she'd thrown herself off the Pont du Diable, but had only succeeded in breaking her legs, so once she was released from the clinic she got someone to drive her up to the monastery at St Florian, where she covered herself in petrol and set herself on fire. Luc was interested in the theological implications of this sequence of events, even though he was a humanist himself. She left a child of four, and the grandparents were now bringing him up as their son. As a result of his partner's retirement, Luc faced the prospect of a full working week in an antiquated surgery, with no records, no equipment, no nurse, no secretary, increased administrative and financial responsibilities and unshared overheads. It had lovely paintings on the wall, and Luc was very popular with his patients, but those were his only assets. Driving up the motorway he said, 'I have to stop painting. I can't do both, not if I have to take over the surgery on my own. I don't want to be a weekend painter.'

'OK,' I said. 'Stop for a bit then. Or take on another associate.'

We drove on a bit further and then he said, 'What about us? How can I live with another artist? Think how you would feel if you couldn't write and you had to go to work all day and I stayed at home and painted.'

I thought I might be quite relieved not to write for a bit; it was such hard work. 'Do you mean that?'

'No. But about the painting, yes.'

He hung the exhibition in the afternoon, and when people started arriving I drove to the station to meet Marcel, who had come down from Paris for the show. Marcel was small, strong, with a big beard and a slash across his chest where they had taken out his heart and reset it the previous year. He always asked me how I was, in a way that had nothing to do with the way people say 'and how are you?' For a Freudian he was a great storyteller, too.

When we got to the gallery, Luc was leaning against a pillar, rolling a cigarette and answering questions. I was surprised he was so relaxed, talking quietly to a crowd of people, not getting irritated when people asked questions he would have refused to answer if they'd come from anyone he knew or expected ever to know better. Anyone who lived in this cold, grey place, with its clammy airs, obviously had to be treated kindly.

The woman who was talking had her back to me and Marcel. She said, 'This is very beautiful work. Such strength and elegance, such expression. Could you tell us what you understand by beauty? Is it very important to you?' Marcel had moved forwards to stand quite close to Luc, and was now facing the speaker as she asked her question. I saw his face fall, then he straightened up, catching himself, and looked anxiously at Luc while feeling around in his pocket for the pipe he had given up after the operation. Luc answered quietly. He said he had no theory on beauty; he just did it like that, he had no strict rules about it. When I came up afterwards, Marcel took my arm and pointed out the woman who had asked the question. Her face was burned almost completely away. It was obvious from the way she was dressed that she was accustomed to appearing in the guise of a beautiful woman. Obvious, also, that the disfigurement was something that had happened very recently. The next morning Luc said to Marcel that he was driving him straight to the station for Paris, that we had to get back down south.

We drove all day and arrived late in the evening. The village was a riot of Catalan flags, bright red and yellow; it was the night of the corrida. During the afternoon the bulls had been killed and there had been sardane dancing in the square. There was a smell of roasting meat, and wine everywhere, flamenco dancers weaving great question marks in the air, with taut fingers and long, supple arms. We got separated in the crowd, but I knew where to find him at two in the morning on corrida night. The woman who lived in the huge house by the war memorial was in her nineties and had known Luc's grandmother as a child. On summer nights she would wander out of her front door in her nightclothes and stop teenagers in the street to ask them the time, over and over. It would bring tears to Luc's eyes, and he would cross the road from the café and go indoors with her and find a chair in the summer house and sit with her. He was always kind to old people, in the way people are who are old enough to remember how their grandparents grew frail and needed them when they were scarcely more than children. His maternal grandfather had crashed his car in front of Les Lauriers restaurant at ten miles an hour and died. Children came running into the surgery ten yards away and shouted, 'Luc, your grandfather's dead.' If Luc ever dies a violent death it will be by strolling into something stationary while whistling with his hands in his pockets, feeling round for a light.

I danced with Stefan, who would always dance, and then joined Luc back at the car. We drove up to the farm, and he stumbled straight out onto the terrace without switching on the light in the living room, and

I knew it was because the piano reminded him of the square bourgeois drawing rooms of Burgundy.

An English girl who lived a few villages away with her husband, a holiday rep, and their small child, rang me the next day and asked me to meet her at the pizzeria for lunch. I'd never met her before. She was sexy and strong, but her face didn't look quite real. Over lunch, as she talked to me about her marriage, her affairs, the spinelessness of men, their scant libidos, the mean things her current lover had said about Luc, I realized she had the face of someone put together by a police artist. The eyes did not quite go with the mouth, the cheekbones were out of balance with her chin and the hair colour wasn't quite right.

'How many lovers have you had since you got married?'

'Since I split up, you mean?'

'No, since you got married, sweetheart.'

'One, I suppose. What about you?'

'Fuck knows,' she said.

She wore a sundress with little pink sprigs, like the ones Irish women try to sell you in underground stations. On her chest, above her swooping breasts, her skin was prickled with heat.

'You should do something about your voice,' she said. 'You sound like a dumb blonde, or a kid.'

'What's up?' Luc asked that night.

'That girl I met.'

'What about her?'

'Something about her. She scared me.'

'Did she make a pass at you?'

'No. Something else. She feels like bad luck. Like she tried to find out something, and I told her and then she left.'

177

'Oh dear. What did you tell her? Some lies?'

I hadn't told her anything, as far as I could remember. Bits and pieces. We'd talked a bit about my ex-husband, about what I thought had been wrong.

'Nothing.'

In the middle of the night Luc switched on the light.

'*Bon, c'est fini,*' he said heavily. 'It's over. Take your things in the morning. Don't ever come back. I never want to see you again.'

After a long silence, in which we both considered what he'd said I asked, 'Why?'

'Don't play games,' he said, 'it's obvious.'

'What?'

'Look', he said, 'you spend two hours raving about a woman who's slept with half the village, then you wake up in the middle of the night and say you've been sleeping with my best friend.'

'Who?'

'Stefan.'

'I slept with Stefan?'

'Apparently.'

'Who says so?'

'You did. Just now.'

'Of course I didn't. That's crazy. I didn't say anything at all.'

'Nothing?'

'Nothing at all.'

'Oh. It must have been a dream then.'

The next day, Sunday, he took his horse and set off without telling me, taking his hat. When he got back a couple of hours later I was playing the piano. I heard the stable door slam, which he never allowed it to do. He came in and flung some rice in a pan. I stopped playing and he told me that both the horses were limping. The vet said it was because there had been too much rain in the spring, and now the grass was too rich and lush, and they were eating so much of it that they had gout. 'There's never been abundance or luxury here before,' he said. I thought of the bishop and the tennis racquets. That evening he asked me to play the third Schubert Impromptu, Brigitte's piece. When I'd finished, he said, 'What is large, black and shiny, and has three legs?'

'The piano,' I said.

'Try again.'

'I don't know. What?'

'The horses,' he said. 'Since the piano arrived they've been lame. Since the piano arrived everything's gone wrong. This isn't my life I'm living, it's yours.'

'That's not true,' I said. 'How can you say that? Everything we do, it's because it's what you do. That's how it seems to me.'

'Ah well,' he said sadly, quieter now. 'We've had it then. *On est foutu.*'

I went to Brittany to see my brother for two weeks, and returned after a thirteen-hour train journey to the most beautiful railway station in the world, where Luc was waiting for me in the car. As we drove home he said almost nothing, except, 'I saw that girl you had lunch with. She was with your husband in the market.' He drew up outside my flat, opposite the Museum of Modern Art, where the flag with his name on still hung, by an oversight, and said, 'It's over. I don't want to see you again.'

Later he said, 'And that was odd, because it hadn't occurred to me it was over till I saw you there and you looked so English, so very like an English girl who played the piano.'

I went home to England. He sold the piano. It was bought by a couple who ran a hotel near the sea, who didn't play themselves but thought their guests might like to. When I thought of it, it made me think of an unravished bride gazing out to sea. Wherever I looked I saw him, somehow. Even though he wasn't there, he wouldn't step back into invisibility. We didn't speak for six months, until one day the phone rang in London and he said, 'OK. I love you, come back.'

5. Visitors

Back Again

Luc leaves his surgery just after twelve o'clock. Before lunch he walks the boulevard once, twice, stopping twice, three times a minute to talk with people he was once in class with, or people he treats, or just everyone who knows him, which is everyone.

As he goes he peppers the village with gossip. He tells stories – about the funeral director who crashed the hearse; the baker who's swallowed a tooth; the ski instructor who jumped off the Pont du Diable; the woman who rinsed, spat, delicately wiped and whispered, '*Embrasse-moi*', breathing a mix of mint and drilled ceramic in his face.

Today he has finished early and is already sitting at a table in the shade with his father, who is an old man now and barely knows where he is, except he could be nowhere else, since the only other place he remembers ever having been was a POW camp in Aachen.

The mayor's wife, Luc's mother's cousin, is standing chatting with him as I cross the square. She leans down and whispers in his ear. The strap of her halter-neck dress has slipped and her darkly speckled shoulder is like a stone. Even his own cousin flirts with him.

'What did she say?' I ask him as I sit down at the table. 'What was she whispering in your ear?'

He imitates her way of hissing her words, as though

she were spraying them onto the skin just below his ear, and then withdrawing quickly, to assess the effect.

' "Marry that girl," ' he whispers. ' "Make her a baby, quick!" '

At lunch, some days, no-one speaks. Others, Luc and his father discuss the family inheritance; old friends who have died; Conchita, the maid; her Spanish resistant husband who has only one lung. Sometimes I just listen and watch. I am always watching him.

Today I'm reading a letter I found in the tin box on the wall on my way out of the house I've recently bought. It is from a woman in North Carolina, who lives in a retirement home, answering an advert I've placed in the *London Review of Books*. Her name is Irene Bishop. She wants to rent the house for three weeks in late October and early November. 'P.S. I am seventy-seven and walk with a stick. Please let me know how the house is heated. Could you get in some wood?'

Luc glances at it when he comes back from paying the bill. 'Tell her no. We don't want to have to bury her. Why won't these old people stay at home? *Quelle époque!*' He is always saying '*quelle époque*' as an aside to his dog, or a horse, or me. But though I write to Irene and tell her the house is really not suitable, that there are too many staircases and only a stove, which has to be fed with wood, and give her, instead, the name of a hotel, she writes back and says a hotel is no way to visit a place. She wants somewhere where she can unpack.

She tells me about herself. The last time she was in France was in the 1950s. Her husband had been work-ing in Europe and their child was born in Paris. She nearly died in childbirth and has been frail ever since. Her husband bolted. She returned to America and taught English literature in New York until she retired to North Carolina. She and her friends in the retirement home started up a reading group. They have just read *Love, Again* by Doris Lessing. She says the most important word in that title is the comma.

When she hears I write books, but that I finished one a year ago and am stuck, when I tell her if I stay now I have to stay for ever, that I miss something I can't put my finger on, that I am sometimes oddly afraid, she sends me an e-mail from her white room in the condominium in North Carolina that says, 'Write. It doesn't matter what you write, just make sure that when the angel comes you're there in front of your keyboard and not busy dusting down shelves or cooking a meal for some man.'

She isn't sure if she will make it to the house – six months is a long time at her age, she says – but she likes to think she might. In the meantime she wants me to write to her about it. She wants to know how to get there, what the house is like, where you can swim, the names of the rivers and the mountains, the opening hours of the shops, the weather, the temperature, history and the things I love best, even, she says, if that includes a man.

I've never believed in muses. They always seem to take the form of some woman in a condition of exquisite passivity, being there for some man who is fulfilling himself as an artist, sticking her down on a chair and tying her hands behind her back. This woman seems like a different kind of muse. I do what she says, and send her letters, with instructions, just in case she needs them later on.

I'd decided to buy a house when I got back to the village. I would always need somewhere not too isolated to work, whatever happened. When I worked up at the

185

farm all day I saw no-one from eight in the morning till eight at night, except the dog, the horses and Luc's crazy brother. My friends thought I was mad to go back at all, but when I stopped off in Paris on the way down Marcel said, 'Off you go. Your story isn't over, yet.'

I said, 'You're a professional. What do you think? People always say it's a mistake to go back.'

He thought about it and said, 'What do you think? Do you think it's a mistake to go back?' Psychoanalysts always do that. It's like getting paid for doing Latin exercises, turning direct statements into questions.

By this time the dental practice had settled into a routine. Luc had bought a computer from a salesman called Didier who lived in the Auvergne. Every time Luc had a problem with his files Didier got in his car and drove 300 kilometres to sort it out. He said Luc was the sort of person who made his profession – his *métier* – worthwhile. A lot of his patients seemed to think Luc made having toothache worthwhile. One woman, an elderly friend of his mother, thought of his surgery so much as home, she kept having slips of the tongue and calling the *salle d'attente* – the waiting room – *la salle de bain*. At each appointment, she said, before she lay down in the dentist's chair, she felt an impulse to undress.

While I was away and Luc was setting up the surgery on his own, he decided never to paint again, and burned every picture he had left. He said he started off just clearing some space out in the barn. Because he painted on plain brown wrapping paper, his pictures were highly combustible. There were two or three he didn't like, so he carried them in a roll down to the bottom of the field and set them alight. They went up with a shoosh into the leaves of the trees which shot in an instant from green to flame to carbon. It was spring. He was spring cleaning.

The fire was going well. He said it looked rather beautiful in the dark, that there was something in the paint that made the flames glow blue, so he went back to the barn to see if there was anything else he could add. There were more rolls in the barn, some of the paintings left over from the show in Burgundy, so he decided to burn those, too. By morning, he said, everything had gone. Everything he had ever painted in fifteen years, apart from what he had sold or what was on show in galleries and museums. He said it was like going to the hairdresser for a trim and ending up with your head shaved.

He had been depressed all winter. Shortly after burning his paintings he'd been sitting around in Gigi's shop, moping, when he abruptly levered himself out of the sofa and said he was going to have a haircut. She thought this was odd at the time, because he usually cut his hair himself. He came back half an hour later with it cut almost to his skull, looking spectrelike and ready for some sacrificial ceremony. *'C'est fini,'* he said, meaning the haircut. Later that evening she became convinced he was going to kill himself and rang Marcel in a panic. Marcel said Luc wasn't the suicidal type and she should stop being such a *maman* to him; he'd only just lost one mother, he didn't need a new one quite yet.

His mother had dropped dead while cooking fish one Saturday lunchtime after the market. *'Plouf!'* he said, in cartoon language, *'Morte!'* It was the day I'd left to go back to England. Luc, who always read the horoscopes in the local paper, told me his mother's had said, 'Beware Le Poisson' – French for Pisces.

'Which is odd,' he said when he told me about it, 'because that's your sign.'

The last time she had knocked on his door, bringing him some pots of apricot jam, he hadn't answered because I was packing and it wasn't the moment. We found the pots of jam on the step later, but he never rang to thank her and never spoke to her again.

When she died he went to Spain and bought a horse.

She was half-Arab, half-back street, and Luc fell in love with her at first sight. He loved anything that was physically irregular. In the surgery he loved treating old people who had lost all but a few of their teeth, and he was the dentist of choice for all the people with Down's syndrome who lived in a home at the end of the valley. They delightedly exchanged drawings and paintings, and Luc loved the way his were indistinguishable from theirs. 'It's a parrot,' his favourite patient, Nicole, would say in a challenging tone, handing him a nonchalant scribble that looked remarkably like one of his own drawings. 'So it is,' he would say, biting his lip, and the two of them would burst out laughing so hard they'd have to slide down the walls and sit on the floor.

He called the horse Chiquita. She was frisky but ugly, a disconcerting combination. She had lost her mother as a foal and had been raised by a human, and she believed she was human, too, not a horse. Sometimes she would come clopping into the house and mooch around the sitting room, nosing among Luc's tax papers. When that happened Luc would say quietly, 'Quick, get the phone off the hook.' The first time this happened I thought it was an odd priority, but he explained later that the phone, an old Seventies model, which pealed so loud you could hear it down the bottom of the field, would have terrified the horse and made her buck and charge into the walls or through the plate-glass window. It wasn't difficult to imagine her sailing through the glass, legs splayed, sprouting wings at the very last moment, soaring away over the mountain. Gigi came to look at her the weekend Luc brought her back. She took one look at her over the green gate and said perhaps he should have called her Clothilde. It's true, she had something of the none-too-bright but willing peasant about her. The first thing he did when I got back was introduce us.

House Buying

I was first shown the house by Monsieur Barthieu, a
small, carefully coiffed Trotskyist. He worked for an
estate agent called Monsieur Dada, for whom he staged
performances, by appointment. I was looking for somewhere small, inexpensive, but with what French estate
agents call 'cachet'. He understood – completely, he
assured me with an off-centre grin – my requirements.
A writer! His mind's eye focused, twitching with
pleasure. He wanted me up in that south-facing room
at a little table, with a view out onto perfectly tended
gardens, with fruit trees and trailing vines and stone
balustrades and a nightingale in the early evening. Do
you write in the morning or the evening? The morning.
Ah. He touched my shoulder with the tip of his pipe.
And in the evening? In the evening, I said, I read and eat.
Ah. I see. You like the sun when you write. Yes, I said, I
like the sun when I write. So he trailed me on that first,
blistering-hot house-hunting morning round a number
of glum properties that were all completely wrong. 'I
know – I can see! – exactly what you are looking for,' he
said. 'We will find it. But I must warn you. It could take
a year, maybe more.' As the bells tolled five to twelve
and we were thinking about breaking for lunch, he
stopped dead in the street. He looked up at the house
with the bulge. 'And yet,' he said, 'and yet . . .'

The woman who answered the door looked like someone who'd retired from the Summer Special Show in 1976, tan, wiry and blonde. She was fiftyish, very thin, and wore leggings and a turquoise T-shirt. Madame does not own the house. We would, therefore, it turned out later, have to consider Madame's interests very carefully. Madame had said the only time prospective buyers could visit the house was at mid-day on Wednesdays – nice timing! – and that she had to be found somewhere to live not only for herself, but for her sixteen cats as well. The house stank of ammonia, like a 1950s hairdressing salon.

Tenants' rights are well protected in France. There was no question of turfing Madame out. After all, said Monsieur Barthieu, you can always live with your boyfriend. But I wouldn't be buying the house if I wanted to live with my boyfriend. Then why is he your boyfriend if you don't want to live with him? Don't you want to have his babies?

He had a way of always asking the awkward questions. Nor was his Trotskyism an empty affair. He was a protector of the interests of the non-property-owning poor. As both Madame and I, at this point, fell into that category, he was an estate agent made in heaven. He sold me the house at a fraction of what it should have cost, and rehoused Madame in an elegant squat on the square.

Madame had been a good tenant for the previous owner, a Belgian psychoanalyst from Bruges. He had met a Japanese widow, living in Paris, at the spa the previous summer. They had married, and decided to sell up in Bruges, Paris and the village so they could buy a bigger house here for their retirement, with a large garden. It's always good to meet people who are planning on a large garden for their retirement. At the time of the negotiations for the house the man had a broken leg, having fallen off a ladder while picking cherries. When I went to see them he was lying on a chaise longue, sipping green tea from thimble cups, looking out at his garden. He told stories about his practice in Bruges, while his new wife reminisced about Regent Street, where she'd bought a Burberry raincoat in the Sixties. If they hear you write books, people tell you stories. You're the one they catch at the gate to the wedding feast, whose coat edge they twitch at, who always, as they know, has a moment and one to spare. They told me Madame, their tenant, had a boyfriend who kept her. He sold spices and African clothing in the Sunday morning market on the coast.

Just before I made the offer on the house, Luc came round to have a look at it. Even though it had been built in 1500, or thereabouts, to him it seemed like a Wimpey home that had just sprung up out of nowhere, since it didn't feature on his personal map of the village, on which only the lines that he had traced himself existed at all. It's only visitors who explore a place. In the place where you were born and brought up you never go looking for things, or trying to get the general picture. He was astonished that he could have lived in the village all his life and have no idea that this perspective existed, this way of looking at the mountain. It was as though he'd had an envelope sitting around for years and I'd one day slit it open and said, 'Look. Go on, take a look at what's inside.'

He said, 'Of course you have to have it. It's perfect for you.' It wasn't perfect, but it was beautiful. You can walk through any pretty village and think how lovely it would be to have a little place there, but it's really rare, in fact, to find somewhere where you feel happy, and where there is enough light.

The day I got the keys and paid the cheque it was

pouring with rain. I said to Luc at breakfast, 'You will help me paint and plaster won't you?'

He poured himself some more coffee and licked the edge of his roll-up thoughtfully. After a while he said, 'No. No, I don't think I will. I've more than enough to do here on the farm really, without helping you with your place.'

I didn't enjoy taking possession. If you go to get a divorce in France, the lawyer will beam across the table at you, surrounded by hugely blown-up photographs of his smiling wife and happy children. If you go to buy a house, you can be sure the photographs of his elegant domain will sour your pleasure at your own meagre acquisition. 'So, Mademoiselle,' he said, 'you were born in nineteen seventy-three.'

'Sixty-three,' I said.

'Sixty-three? No!' He clutched at imaginary beads at his chest, like a duchess in a pantomime. 'Surely not!' He opened his palms to the sellers, he in plaster and she in her serviceable Burberry for special occasions. 'I appeal to you, Messieurdames, is it possible? Surely not. But never mind. Your little house will give you plenty of grey hairs, I am sure. Cracks do not always appear first on the surface. When you come to sell it we will say, so, you were born in nineteen forty-three, Mademoiselle.'

I signed the cheque, which was enormous. It was the size of a magazine or a certificate for doing well at ballet class. I had to sign it and have it countersigned by the lawyer, who then presented it to the owners. I found it difficult to take as much pleasure in this little ritual as the lawyer himself seemed to do. I thought ritual was meant to be a way of cushioning an act, of providing a cathartic release of tension. But this was just a lawyer handing over a huge cheque with my name on it to someone who would later go and pay it into their own account.

It was pouring with rain. I walked up into the old village with the two keys, one tiny and one barely portable, in my rucksack. It was December. I couldn't remember why I'd bought the house. It took all the money I had in the world. I had no regular income. This was the place I was supposed to be forgetting. I loved Luc, but I felt he was bad for me, that he appealed to my rather base instinct towards the cleverest, best-looking, funniest boy in the class, who would boost my confidence then let me down. I had a subconscious system for recognizing these men. Every time I started going out with one I would dream about a boy at school who was clever and handsome and good at sport, and who had never noticed me at all, though I was glued to him in my head and we were scheduled to marry. It took me ages to realize that the subconscious meant the dream as a warning, not a prompt. England was only a few hours away. I had been searching for something to decide for me whether I wanted to go home or stay. I had found it. I had just paid £30,000 I didn't have for it. It was an expensive way to flick a coin.

It was almost lunchtime. Henri, the cardiologist, stopped and offered me a lift.

'I've got another story for you,' he said cheerily. 'It's on the back seat in the plastic folder. Usual drill. Don't feel you have to be kind.' Henri dropped me in the corner of the car park and said he'd come round after work and mend the window in the top bedroom. It breaks whenever a wind from the north slams the bedroom door. It just crumbles and falls to the floor.

I let myself into the house and dropped the big key into a bucket in the kitchen. I looked at all the places that were dripping. I noted all the long cracks in the outside supporting walls. I hadn't had a surveyor in to check. It would be arrogant, Monsieur Barthieu had seemed to suggest, to suppose that after withstanding centuries of pestilence, sun and rain, it was going to develop a fatal fissure just for me. You couldn't even see out of the foggy window at the view that had made me fall in love with the house the previous August. My head span and sang from the cat smell of diluted ammonia, which was acting like a eucalyptus chest rub and emptying my sinuses. I sat down on the floor in the kitchen, in the middle, where it seemed least likely I'd see a rat, and read Henri's story about a girl in a red bikini on the beach in July.

In my life I've met three medical doctors who've shown me their pornographic stories. It must be almost time for an anthology. I didn't mind reading Henri's stories because they were rather good, and because, I'm afraid, he was so attractive. Henri had such astonishing eyes that if he'd ever run amok and you'd stopped someone in the street and said, 'Did you see a man carrying a chainsaw dripping blood run past here twenty seconds ago?' they'd say, 'Oh, the one with the blue eyes? He went that way.' Later on, Henri came round and mended the window very slowly, using putty and a square-ended knife, and it continued to rain.

But after a few weeks of cloud and mist and more rain, I walked into the house one morning when the sun shone and thought, This is where I meant to come after all. Now I realized that the sun hit the terrace before I even woke, so that when I stumbled down the stairs to the kitchen, made my coffee and took it outside to drink, the seats of the chairs and the stones and the terracotta tiles were already warm.

The house had hidden itself from me successfully for the first few weeks, pretending not to be what it was. It was the lover glimpsed at an airport or on a passing ship, who returns disguised as a fat merchant or a beggar to test the strength of your love. It had come to me with all its charm cast off, wanting me to love it for the disposition of its rooms, the things that still work when the sun doesn't shine, its smell of old wood, its secret cupboards and staircase laid with terracotta tiles. Once I'd proved, grudgingly, my affection, it came to me undisguised and turned out to be even better than I'd thought.

Mild Xenophobia

A man called Serge Collier, who had once been a type-
setter for the Presses Universitaires de France, fixed all
the leaks and cracks. He would work for a day and a
half, then stop for a week. He and his second wife had
fostered two small children – twins – who had come
from a home neither of them remembered. Serge sat
out on my terrace for hours, smoking calmly, talking
about women, children, politics and his frustrated love
affair with his wife.

The walls were pitted and crevassed, and bulged in
places. I covered them in white lime – *chaux* – bought
from the paint shop in the village by the sackload, and
the effect was as flattering as snow. It scuffed so easily
that it soon looked as though a herd of elephants had
had an all-night romp in the arctic, but it didn't matter
because the lime was cheap and easy to reapply.

I painted the woodwork grey-blue, the colour of all
woodwork in old houses in the south, since the colour
is said to repel flies. The wooden floors soaked up
beeswax from a rectangular yellow tin, a product
whose packaging hadn't been redesigned since the turn
of the century. I found that if you waxed the floors just
before lunch, they caught the sun just as you finished,

197

and to polish them you could skate around with cloths tied to your feet with twine, and execute double salchows with lighting effects that didn't rely on having sequins sewn on your socks. Luc would arrive at midday and say, 'You're making a good job of it. It's important to do it yourself. Otherwise, before you know where you are, everyone will start to call it "Luc's house".'

It was the most pathetic reason I'd ever heard for not picking up a paintbrush. 'Why on earth should they do that? It's my house. Yours is up there.'

'Because the village is like that.'

'No, it's not. Only you are. Stop saying the village when you mean you.'

'*Le village, c'est moi.*'

'You'd better be kidding,' I said.

I needed to let the house out over the summer to pay the mortgage, hence the advert in the *London Review of Books*, who have a perfect classified ads section. I always turned to the back page before ploughing through the essays on William Empson or politics in early seventeenth-century Rome. Their classifieds so exactly reflect the readership that you could feel kinship with the people who wrote on William Empson and the rest, simply by desiring what they desired: a two-bedroom house in Highgate, a room for writing in Brooklyn, an out-of-print edition of poems. Now they have a personal ads column it has become a bit more difficult to dream along with them. I found it easier to get excited about 'House on Missolonghi Peninsula, view of temple, vegetable garden, £70 a week' than about 'Shy, ugly man, fond of extended periods of self-pity, middle-aged, flatulent and over-weight, seeks the impossible'. I'd love to know if he found it, though.

The advert said that the house was for rent by the

week from May to September, that it was 25 kilometres from the sea, on the Spanish border, that it was sunny and in a village. The rent was too cheap, but I didn't want the kind of people who were going to worry when the door handles fell off. I was lucky. Every person who came to stay in the house, including Irene herself, was the kind of person who brought, and left behind, something rich and often strange.

Holidays are special instances of how the shutter can open for a second's worth, a week or two in a longish life, when colour and light and shape and shadow burn into the liquid film and are fixed. When people come to your house, to a new place, on the strength of a three-line advert, you hand over an image from which endless prints can be made, different every time. For each family, or couple or group of friends, the place shifted and rearranged itself. First impressions last only a couple of days; after three days the main street starts to look different, a sense of the whole modifies the first encountered part.

I envied them that first period of disorientation, when the ordinary still looked unusual and strange. It's a gift some painters and writers have of perceiving the foreignness of the everyday and of existence, of being as disoriented in the world as visitors to a new place, experiencing the same sense of unsureness as a motorist trying to drive through a narrow gap. I always thought that hymn 'New Every Morning Is The Love' must be about that. Every day new, asking for an accommodation of the heart to what had grown un-familiar overnight. All the interesting people I've known have loved to travel to new places.

Except Luc. He would never move unless he had to. He considered the desire to travel a sign of weakness, the way primary-school teachers regard not being able to sit still. He despised Angélique of Papillon Vert because she kept a picture of a beach in the Dominican Republic taped above the toasted-sandwich maker in her café to keep her going. He disliked the way time was now divided between work and leisure. He would have liked a life in which work was leisure and leisure, work. You could be a shepherd, I suggested. 'Or a writer,' he replied. The work/leisure divide was particularly acute in cities. He had no time for people who lived '*en ville*'. '*Ils sont cons*,' he would say, and shake his head and chuckle at their absurdity. I pointed out that a) people needed jobs b) most people had to live in cities if they wanted work and c) not everyone had the luck to be born in a beautiful place, and the inherited wealth to stay there even if they were.

'Do I live like a king? Do I ask for much? Anyone would say I lived in virtual poverty. I eat rice and eggs, and grow my own vegetables and my own hay.'

'Yes,' I'd say, 'but you need a big estate to do that. You don't get depressed eating rice and eggs because you do it sitting on your terrace at sunset with your horses munching down below, a bottle of wine that cost 5 francs, or nothing, and cheese one of your patients has given you and fruit from your trees. Of course it costs you nothing. You can afford to be poor.'

It was important not to look like a tourist. Anyone who did was committing the double felony of being on holiday and not being '*d'ici*'. Luc and his friends would always blink at foreigners who ran around wearing shorts. I'd say, but look how comfortable they are. You've all got sweat running down the inside legs of your jeans. '*On n'est pas à la plage*,' they would say. '*On est en ville.*' It showed a lack of respect, toy-town treatment. Did the English wear shorts in their own country? Their own towns? To go shopping? I said that in the same way as English architects had got back from the Costa Brava in the Seventies and built white block houses to deflect the sun, English designers had come back with the sun in their eyes and run up shorts for us to walk round our white block houses in, and now we'd seize any opportunity to wear them, appropriate or not. It was all part of the travel boom; the world getting smaller.

'Ah, *le global village*,' they said, glumly, a phrase they had picked up from reading *Le Monde*. In the global village, in cyberspace, everyone was a tourist. That was the *style de l'époque*: dipping in, dipping out; popping up here, vanishing there; sampling and discarding; dabbling and appropriating.

So when my visitors arrived he would feel sad for them, these Englanders, that their own country wasn't good enough, that they were 'on holiday', and when he saw them photographing each other on the café terrace or under the plane trees, it seemed to him they were faking something, like when you stick your head into the gap left for a face in the wooden cut-out of a muscle man or a *fille des Folies Bergères* at a fairground. He would nod at them, embarrassed in front of his friends that he was responsible, through me, for introducing these strangers onto the streets.

I did my best, by speaking little and sticking my head in a newspaper whenever I was at the café, not to betray my nationality. It wasn't that I didn't want to be English. I just didn't want to be English in France. Frenchwomen said that Englishmen were all either neanderthals or they looked like Prince Charles, and no wonder so many English women went out with Frenchmen. I knew this was rubbish, and that Ralph Fiennes was the best-looking man in the world, but they had only seen *The English Patient*, and remembered him with his face burned away, so it was a difficult argument to sustain.

The older French, in particular, didn't even pretend

to like the English. During the week of the fiftieth anniversary celebrations of the D-Day landings, when Clinton, Mitterrand and the Queen posed for pictures on the beach in Boulogne, and complicated coastal maps were shown on the evening news, Luc's mother said over lunch, 'I don't know why they invited the Queen of England. After all, the English did nothing in the war, just kept themselves to themselves and looked after their own till the Americans stepped in, and now they try to claim some glory from it. Have they got no shame?'

I mentioned the Battle of Britain, the Blitz and Dunkirk, trying not to sound like someone Mrs Thatcher would have invited to sit on a conference platform.

'Yes, yes,' she said, 'we know all about that. What about the number of boys from this village who were killed getting British airmen across the border?' I stared at my grated carrots and courgettes and I thought, Why didn't they teach me enough at school so that I'd know what to say now? How come I know what kind of crockery the ancient Egyptians ate their millet out of, but I can't win this argument in one simple sentence?

Luc raised his eyebrows at me, and said, '*Maman*,' in a warning voice. He told me afterwards that most people round here – unlike the northern French – liked to make out the British had behaved selfishly in World War Two. The south had little respect for their own role, but at least they had suffered a semi-occupation. Britain didn't even endure that. It was false and absurd, but it helped them to believe it. It's a provincial French reflex to scorn the English, just as the English like to scorn the French. It makes you realize what it feels like to belong to a minority group. It feels just like being bullied at school, except that it usually happens behind your back. They excused themselves by saying that, of course, I was exempt from their generalizations, an exception to the rule. Luc would say to me, 'You're OK, you're more French than English anyway,' and I'd think, No, I'm not. Whenever Britain made some pronouncement on Europe I knew about it before I read it in the paper because people would stop me in the street and say, 'What on earth is wrong with you all?'

One Saturday in May I was introduced to a man sitting with Luc when I came back from the chicken van at the end of the market. I sat down beside him and he began flirting, and soon discovered I wasn't French. 'Dutch? Swedish?' he enquired, coquettishly. 'No,' I said, '*Anglaise.*'

'I knew you were,' he said. 'You only have to look at your skin colour. White!' He chuckled. 'Red in summer!'

'Excuse me,' I said, 'but if you look, my arm is dark brown. You must be confusing it with your own.' He had placed his arm very close to mine on the arm of his chair, and it was piglet pale. He drew backwards sharply, clutched his arm to his chest as though I'd just poured boiling water onto it. He shook his fist in my face. Luc stopped his conversation on the other side of the table and cocked his head.

'That,' said the irate Frenchman, jabbing at my arm, 'is the skin of an Englishwoman who has finished tanning. And that,' pointing at his own pale flesh, 'is a Frenchman who has not yet even begun.'

Marnie

Many of those who came to stay in the house were old but very lively. There was a couple who arrived at the end of the morning market, and went and ate for two hours at Les Lauriers. They announced themselves at the house mid-afternoon, smelling sweetly of golden Rivesaltes wine and some fruity dessert, having met half the village already. He had been widowed and had nine children. She'd been his student. I followed them around with my eyes, thinking, That's it, that's love. Don't settle for less. Don't mistake anything else for that. Luc said they were *alcoolos*, and he hoped they wouldn't peg out while they were staying in my house, because he was sure I wasn't insured for the death of people I wasn't related to. He said the same thing when a couple arrived from Suffolk, both well into their eighties, reminding me of John Bailey and Iris Murdoch, or what I thought I knew of them then. They had been driving through Suffolk in the early 1970s, they told me, and had seen a for-sale sign outside a deserted priory. They had gone in and explored, and decided they had to live there. So they got together as many friends as they could, and they bought it collectively and had been running it as a free-thinking commune for over twenty years. And there was Marnie, whom I scarcely met.

Marnie was the first person to come to the house. I had just put the advert in the paper and was in London, organizing a removal van. I was so sick of packing, I decided I would never move countries again, that it was too much trouble. Duncan said that when David and Frieda Lawrence moved about all they took with them were some books, but only the essential ones – how did they decide? – and some rolled-up carpets they'd bought in Africa. Whenever they arrived somewhere, Duncan said, they just *flung* these carpets down on the floor, after Frieda had been round with the broom, of course, and they immediately felt at home. She left her children behind and took two carpets. I'd rationalized my stuff right down to what I thought was a bare minimum, but the bare minimum still seemed to include things like the second edition of the *Collins Guide to Animal Spoors* in Danish. One day, I believed, it would really come into its own, when someone from Copenhagen was trying to identify a species of boar in the woods. I had files full of parking tickets from the 1980s, because I had the idea that they were like bank statements, if you kept them for seven years and then burned them something magic would happen, a flimsy redemption of a wings and glitterdust nature, which would be denied you if you carelessly threw them away.

I was packing up boxes when the phone rang. I thought at first the woman on the other end of the line had got the wrong number and was actually trying to get through to the Samaritans. Her voice was cauterized, deep, as though some of the cables were cut. She said she and her husband were decorating a house in London. She said she had to get away somewhere quickly and she'd seen my advert, and could she go, even though it was April and the ad was for May. I said there was hardly any furniture and only a few plates and glasses, but if she was desperate and didn't mind a mess then it was fine by me. She said she'd go the following day, a Monday. How could she get there?

I told her to fly to Barcelona or Gerona, and from there get a train to Figueras. I don't know why I said that. I knew it was really difficult to get from Figueras across the border to the town, but until you got to Figueras it was so incredibly easy and quick and cheap that it broke your heart to go the long way, on the train via Paris or the plane to Toulouse. The trouble was that, after Figueras, you really were stuck. But she spoke Spanish, so I said maybe there'd be a bus. I gave her Luc's number at the surgery and told her to call him if she got into trouble.

Two days later Luc rang me. I was still packing boxes. Marnie had called him from Figueras at midday to say there was no bus. He was just finishing putting a crown on someone's incisor and was about to go off to the pizzeria for lunch.

He drove to Figueras and picked her up. She had an extremely heavy bag, and round her waist she wore a leather belt with great big studs, like a bulldog's, which turned out to have some prosthetic function because she'd fallen off a wall at a rock concert as a teenager and damaged her back. She was still in constant pain from the injury. He drove her to the village, dropped her at the café and then said he had to go back to work. He gave her the keys to his Land-Rover and said she could fetch her suitcase out of the back when she wanted, and keep the keys, as long as she got them back to him at the surgery by seven. Seven o'clock came and there were no keys. He went to the house, and it was all opened up, as though someone was there, but no-one answered the bell. He went to the car park and checked the car was there. Then he started walking the boulevard, thinking he would see her and be able to recover the car keys. No sign. He went to have his pizza, then doubled back to the house around eight thirty. Still no answer, though someone had returned and closed the shutters. He decided to make one more tour of the village before giving up and going to borrow his father's car. As he came back to the car park and was about to turn left down the Rue St Florian to his father's house, he recognized a famous poet who lived in Paris walking towards him down the street. The poet stopped at the café table, and Luc now realized Marnie had been sitting there for some time, probably with his car keys on the table in front of her, by her glass of beer.

'She looked like you,' he said. 'I think I'd thought it was you, even though I knew you were in England. It didn't register, either, that it couldn't be you because you weren't there, or if it was you it was surprising and I would want to go and sit down with you. And it didn't occur to me that if it wasn't you it must be her, and she was the person I was looking for, because it didn't look like her at first, it looked like you.'

By the time he'd thought all this she had walked off up the road with the poet, talking as though they knew each other. They got into a car with a Parisian number plate and drove away.

The next morning, when Luc bumped into Marnie in the street, she produced his car keys from a pouch on her leather belt. They went for lunch, and she told him about the book she was translating from the French, which had originally been translated from Arabic. Luc found the news that she was also translating the lyrics of the songs of Serge Gainsbourg a bit of a disappointment. He didn't ask her about the poet, and she didn't volunteer anything, though she told him about other aspects of her life: her marriage to a singer who was at home decorating the house they were going to sell –

though now I can't remember if it was because they were getting together again or splitting up – her work, her time as a rock groupie, her travels in the Middle East. Luc was fascinated by Marnie, and I was surprised that he didn't leave me for her, but I suppose he thought I was difficult enough, and she was the concentrate form of me. His friends were beginning to think he had some kind of trade going in thin literary English women with uncommonly brown legs, and Stefan was hopping mad.

I took the train from Waterloo station early on the morning after the Labour election victory. The removal lorry had left a few days previously and was due to arrive the following evening in the village, on its way down to the south of Spain. It was odd leaving Waterloo in bright sunshine on a happy morning. A man in his late forties sat opposite me, and next to me was a girl, who turned out to be his daughter. He kept rubbing his hands together gleefully. It was like being in the front row at the Epworth Amateur Dramatic Society's first rehearsal when one man has already, irritatingly, learned the whole of his part. The rest of us were burying our heads in our newspapers. His daughter, who looked about twelve, was reading *Nineteen*.

'Get you some clothes in Paris,' he said. 'Christ,' hand rubbing, 'eighteen years of Conservative rule. Still can't believe we did it. Melissa? Can you?'

Melissa turned a page without looking up. 'I actually have a new *pleated* skirt,' she said. 'Mummy got it in Bath.'

When we came out of the tunnel he said, 'What French do you know?'

'*Je suis en train de lire mon feuilleton,*' she said heavily. '*On est dans le train.*'

'What's your French teacher's name?'

'Miss Armstrong,' said Melissa.

'Miss Armstrong! She nice then?'

'Very.'

Enraged by Melissa's ability, like her mother's, I guessed, to wound him while flicking coolly through a magazine, he reached over and tried to rip it from her. It was an extraordinarily violent gesture. She dodged it, keeping her eyes on the page, and he sagged back, defeated, in his seat.

'Miss Armstrong has a lover who's French,' said Melissa quietly. 'He's very poor. She gives him all her salary and buys him sausages.'

Luc met me at the station and wrapped his arms around me. He had a lovely way of making it clear that, for him, I had come home, that he and the dog were waiting for me, and the horses, and that now I'd moved my things out of England we could settle down to our summer, our life, together.

We arrived back in the village at nine o'clock at night and drove up the street that ran behind Luc's father's house, a quiet, narrow street, with an intersection where you could turn left for the bull ring or right for the Rue St Florian. We had intended to drive straight through, but the intersection was blocked by a huge, long, white lorry. It was the biggest thing I had ever seen in the village. Slowly Luc stopped the car. I think we both had the feeling we were seeing something that had arrived by night and was not meant to be seen by other people, some kind of visitation, an apparition. I felt full of apprehension. The piano had come in such a lorry. There was a full moon, almost. We got out of the car and walked towards it. Luc said happily, '*Qu'est-ce que c'est beau*,' admiring its simple Le Corbusier lines.

Two men were leaning against the cab, smoking

cigarettes in the moonlight. One of them was the spitting image of Fred West. They had brought my possessions. For the moment, we decided, it could all go in Luc's father's garage. It looked like jumble. Just as we were finishing, Marnie arrived, clutching a white pack of Silk Cut extra mild, so she looked as though she might be connected in some way, thematically, with the van – gaunt, and as though if you bent her in two she would snap at the waist.

'Look,' Luc said, pointing her out. 'Isn't she like you?' She said her husband was arriving the following morning to take her home. She had disappeared the last few days, she said to Luc. Some Portuguese friends of hers had been doing a gig in Tarragona and she'd gone to hear them. The Arabic translation was nearly finished. Luc said to me afterwards, 'She wanted to know so much about you.' She kept asking, 'Is she beautiful?' as though that would make all the difference. She had a bruised look about her that made you think of someone carrying heavy suitcases down unsuitable dirt tracks and brushing away flies.

She left the next morning. Luc and I had come down to the market to buy supplies because we were going off riding for a couple of days. I saw her slipping round a corner in a short white skirt, her feet bound up in complicated sandals, with a very tall man at her side, holding her hand. Two days later I got back from the riding trip and let myself into the house. It was quite late at night, and I listened to the messages on the answerphone while standing at the doors onto the terrace. There was a dark, heavy blue sky, with star stitches in it and a lemon moon rising behind the hill, where Luc would be brushing down the horses and leading them into the field for the night. A woman's voice on the tape spoke to Marnie, and the address was so direct it was unnerving. It reminded me of those scenes in films where someone is writing a letter and you hear the words in their voice, making you jump, because you feel you have woken inside them and that you are at the source of their thought. The girl had a deep grazed sort of voice, like Marnie's. She said where she was, in London, the sky was dramatic and sad, that there were great clouds rolling over the moon, and she could see all the lights of London and wasn't sure if it was them or the moon that was lighting the clouds. She said she had filled in Marnie's ballot paper in her absence, as she'd been instructed to do. She left long pauses. She said, 'I don't know, maybe you're there, babe, listening to me. Maybe you've gone.' The tape wound slowly forward, while she thought, or struggled to speak. 'You're not coming back, are you?' There was one more long silence, then the voice said fiercely, tenderly, 'I love you.' When I heard the words I gasped, because I'd never heard them said like that. I suppose you rarely hear someone say 'I love you' to someone else and know it's real, not just acting. Hardly ever, in fact.

Wedding

Marie-Lou eventually convinced Christophe of the fiscal advantages of marriage. The phone rang one Saturday morning and it was Christophe asking Luc to be his best man. Luc was thrilled. He bought them a huge book on the history of the theatre as a wedding present, and ironed his shirt. Gigi rang and said all the female friends were clubbing together to buy Marie-Lou a special wedding present, a surprise. What? The dress, she said. Barbara's already given me a thousand francs. I told Luc I thought it was wrong for Gigi and the other women to buy Marie-Lou's dress, especially as Gigi stood to make a profit from it.

'Look on the bright side,' he said. 'At least you won't have to wear it now.'

On the morning of the wedding I asked Luc what time he needed to be there. Oh, three thirty, he said. Don't you need to get there early? No, he said, just when it begins. He didn't want to ring Christophe to check, because he didn't want to disturb him at a busy time. It seemed a bit odd. Why couldn't he just ring to make sure what was expected of him, and at what time? Instead he rang Gigi, and she said oh, definitely, the wedding began at four. Her boyfriend had ordered them a special silver Cadillac.

We went to Luc's father's house after lunch with our

clothes, ready to change into. At a quarter to four I came to fetch Luc from in front of the television, where he was watching the Tour de France with his father and the poodle. There's plenty of time, he said, it's only three minutes away. We left the house at three minutes to four and arrived at the *mairie* at four exactly, to find a huge crowd in front of it, and Christophe and Marie-Lou climbing into the silver Cadillac, Gigi fluttering confetti over the car and blowing kisses in their wake. Luc said, '*Je m'en fous*' – it's only a ceremony. When Gigi came weaving over to us, I ducked away as she leaned to kiss me and said, 'No thanks, I've already got my make-up on,' because she always left a huge lipstick print on my cheek. Men look foolish with lipstick prints on their cheeks, somehow. It's never, under any circumstances, chic. Rubbing at his crossly with his sleeve, Luc said, 'What time did you say?'

'Three thirty,' she said. 'Darling, Christophe is absolutely livid. I doubt whether Marie-Lou will ever speak to you again.' In fact, Marie-Lou was very gracious about it, and said Gigi had achieved an impressive double, getting back at two of her favourite lovers in one go. The reception was held in their garden. Amelia was the bridesmaid.

Luc was broody. I was talking to Joe, an English friend who was magnificently tipsy, along with Selina, his French wife, who was small and bullet sexy and never wore any make-up and had very firm opinions. She hated Luc. I told them I had come back from Barcelona the previous day, and had hitched a lift on the road between Figueras, where the train dropped me off, and the village. An old man had screeched to a halt at the roadside and said he could take me over the border. He set off driving down the middle of the road, then swerved to the left. I screamed as I saw a huge lorry bearing down on us, dust rolling, and he laughed, filling the car with billowing alcohol fumes, so that I imagined that if we did collide with the lorry we'd ignite and burst cloud high in flames. Just at the last moment he swerved and avoided the lorry, then got back on course for the next one. I was still screaming, but he didn't understand French and I couldn't remember any Spanish, so I yelled, 'STOP!' He laughed. I grabbed the steering wheel just as we were about to disappear under a Dutch juggernaut, and the car span and stopped dead in the dust in a ditch. For a couple of horrible seconds I couldn't work out the central locking system, then I did, and I tumbled out of the car into the road. He pulled off at top speed and was soon round the corner, gone. I was shaking like a wet dog who'd fallen into a freezing lake in winter, though it was a scorching July day. I got to a petrol station, found some Spanish coins and rang Stefan. Eventually he managed to sort out what I was saying and said, 'Wait, I'll be there.' When his car drew up half an hour later, he held me till I'd finished shaking, then drove me slowly home on tiny roads and dropped me at the green gate of the farm. Luc said it was stupid to hitch on that stretch of road near the border – only prostitutes did it there.

When I told Joe and Selina this story at the wedding picnic, Selina shook her head slowly, turned her black chip eyes on me and said, 'I don't believe you.' She said there was something in the way I'd told the story that didn't ring true. She said, 'Either it didn't happen, or you weren't as frightened as you say.' Meanwhile, her husband was watching Luc talking to Gigi under a tree, and he said, 'Do whatever you like for now with that man, but never marry him and never have his children.'

Parents

Luc said maybe we should get married and try to start a family. Then he said maybe we should wait till my next book was published, the one I'd gone to London to sign for. Whenever my agent rang it unsettled him for hours afterwards. He said she had a voice like a woman in an airport. I developed terrible stomach pains and had to go to the doctor, who demonstrated to me how to stand balanced on a plank of wood with two rolling cylinders underneath. He said it would cure my equilibrium problems, and with it my stomach pains, but it didn't.

My parents came out to stay, and met Luc for the first time. Serge Collier, the odd-job man with the fostered twins, gave my parents a basket and a ladder each and took them cherry picking. On their last evening we met up in Luc's father's house. Luc had rung him and told him to put some champagne in the fridge. My parents were stunned by the house, all the lace and mahogany and the Mirós on the walls, and this fine, stammering man with his energetic poodle, who tried to remember the gestures his wife would have made to welcome the future parents-in-law, whose Britannic genes might one day be mingled with his own.

Luc said, 'Papa, where are the glasses?'

His father looked puzzled. My father looked a bit

puzzled, too, standing there reading a framed letter hanging on the wall of the sitting room from a widower who had summoned the doctor one day and left this letter pinned to the front door: 'I have decided to end my life this afternoon; in the interest of good order and in order to cause minimum disruption in the lives of those I leave behind, including yours, good doctor, I shall hang myself in the shower, thus conserving the corpse intact for scientific research.'

Luc's father produced some glasses, the ones we usually drank out of, which were originally mustard jars, the kind with a red plastic lid, and perfect for drinking wine.

'No, papa,' Luc said, 'the champagne glasses. *Maman* had champagne glasses, remember?'

His father pointed vaguely at the cabinet on the wall. There? Luc went over and opened it. No, there were only plastic beakers from the beach house. Try under the book case there? No, these were whisky glasses. The third cabinet? No, there were the family skulls, powdered with gold leaf. Luc's father got the maid to retrieve incisors, canines and the odd molar from the bin in the surgery for him when she was doing her evening clean, and he would insert them into the jaw bone and fix them with superglue.

Luc passed his hand over his face and came up smiling, saying, 'Papa, you've put the incisors where the canines should be.'

His father waved a plastic beaker. 'Let's make do with these; it tastes the same.' But Luc wouldn't give up: 'How about the cupboard over there by the window with the key?'

'No,' his father said quickly. 'Not there; there's nothing there.' Luc turned the key, and inside we found champagne glasses balanced high, stacked in pyramid form, etched with patterns, grey with age, but dozens of them. He took five of them out, wiped them with a cloth and we drank the champagne.

My parents left the next day, waving cheerily and saying, 'See you next month!' when Luc and I planned to go to Scotland. He'd been to Britain once before, on the Eurostar, having flown up to Paris. His plane had been delayed by an incident at the local airport. Another plane, flying in cash for one of the banks in the village, had been held up at gunpoint in an extremely well-organized heist. Stepping off the train he was radiant, because he'd seen Battersea Power Station from the window of the train and stepped out into the new station at Waterloo. '*C'est magnifique!*' he said, gazing up at the web of blue girders. But he hated everything else after that, and within forty-eight hours was demanding to go home. The next day, in Paris, he bought a paper and discovered one of his patients had killed himself. He was an employee at the bank whose money had been stolen, had two small children and was building a swimming pool in his back garden. '*C'est une coïncidence,*' Luc said darkly.

At the café on the evening my parents left, he was grinning with relief: '*Tiens.* I have news.'

'What?'

'I'm not going to Scotland! I'm not leaving here. You go if you want to. See your friends.'

'But I want to go with you.'

'*Tant pis pour toi,*' he said, 'If I start doing things like that there'll be no end to it. I'm staying here.'

Corrida

The corrida came and went. Stefan built a wooden stall in the street and served drinks from it for seventy-two hours non-stop to raise money for the tennis club, while Luc, who was fed up with Stefan's carping, walked up and down in front of the stall and said, 'Oh, look, Stefan's become a shopkeeper at last.'

Stefan no longer considered himself my friend. He said he was really only nagging me to sleep with him out of politeness, and it wasn't as much fun any more. It's difficult when your friend does something irrational for love, particularly when you believe it will make them unhappy in the long run. '*C'est un pauvre petit con*,' he said of Luc. He was angry with me because I had gone back to Luc, I believed in love, and worried about money and work. And I was angry with him because he lived with a woman he loved, who earned his keep while he played tennis all day and slept with women he fell for because of the way they walked their dog or leaned on a bar when ordering a coffee.

Stefan ought to have been passionately opposed to the bull-fight, but found a splendidly casuistic defence for it, saying it was basically a democratic sport, which combined elegance, fair play and respect for the beast. Instead, if Stefan opposed anything, it was sanctimoniousness and vegetarians. He said there was no point in being a vegetarian unless you loved meat and blood. Nothing was worth giving up unless you were passionately drawn towards it, as Nietzsche had been passionately drawn towards God. He admired physical prowess of any kind, and he thought ritual was a good thing. In his role as Mr Testosterone, he always bought a cheap ticket and sat in the full blaze of the sun.

Every year Luc declared that he wouldn't go to the bullfight, that he'd had enough of all that macho crap, that he wasn't interested in what went on in the village anyway, he'd outgrown it when he was about eight and a half; it was an event for neo-villagers, and he loathed the corrida because of the risk to the picadors' horses and the way they were dressed up in ribbons and fluttering strips of paper, like a birthday cake. Every year, on the day of the corrida, he'd go down to the Saturday morning market and come back with two tickets his father had pressed into his hand, always for seats in the shade, – his father, once the official corrida doctor, was given expensive tickets for free. So we always found ourselves bang opposite Stefan, who would keep an eye on me, across the sand circle, to see if I flinched when the sword drove in.

The corrida takes place on the first weekend after *le quatorze juillet*, the national holiday to celebrate the storming of the Bastille. On the day itself, the mayor gives a heart-warming speech in the Place de la Liberté and a brass band marches round the town. It's like a scene out of a Jacques Tati film, as though for a day the village is prepared to pretend to be a normal small French town, trumpeting allegiance to *l'état* and fluttering the tricolour. Then, the minute it's over, out come the Catalan flags, stripes of yellow and red, and the brass trumpets and bugles are put away to make room for reedier instruments and the four-stringed double bass.

Preparations begin early in the year, organized by the bullfighting committee, a butcher, the garage mechanic, a doctor – not the vegetarian Buddhist – and a few others. The members of the committee are all aficionados. People say the red silk sashes they wear round their waists are meant to restrain any physical manifestations of macho excitement due to their temporary elevation to positions of power, and to the scent of blood and the sight of women fainting. As the whole thing seems to be about something oversized, overexcited and engorged with blood trying to escape a tight circular enclosure, it seems like an appropriate reflection of the central idea.

At the Salle de Spectacle, on a rainy evening towards the end of April, the aficionados had shown a video of the bulls grazing peacefully in their landscape in southern Spain. Afterwards the owner of the stud farm declared that these were the most powerful bulls ever to be fought in a village arena. Although the village has a very small bullring compared to the two other major arenas, at Nîmes and Béziers, the committee always brings in giant-sized bulls; they seem to get bigger every year. It isn't done to make your opposition to the event – it's never referred to as a sport – too manifest, but it's fine to pass comment on the inappropriateness of the size of the bulls, to say it is dangerous, will end badly, is a sign of *démesure*. El Manolo was there, too, a tiny torero with a huge reputation. Like footballers, toreros wear good suits and write books. El Manolo was an Eric Cantona of the bullring, given to aphorisms which didn't translate well. I first read about the corrida in a book called *Pour Pablo*, written by a famous torero called Dominguin. He wrote that there must be something sublime about it for a man to be prepared to dress up in pink stockings on a Saturday afternoon in the atomic age to go and fight a bull. They call the pink of the bullring 'Picasso pink'. El Manolo, too, had written his autobiography, a philosophical work about the atavistic origins, the Jungian significance of his art. It also talks a lot about his sex drive.

The corrida begins at five in the afternoon. There is not much that begins at five in the afternoon. It is after siesta and before early mass. The start is heralded by solemn music and is punctual to the second. A hush drops over the crowd as the all-male procession comes out into the arena, and people stop wriggling and craning their necks to see who has come with whom. There is an uneasy, semi-religious atmosphere. Knowing that you are here to witness a sacrificial death creates intimacy. There is no possibility of pretence. You could not have come here by mistake. It generates the same feeling of nervous unease I have always felt when taking Communion among friends with whom I rarely attend church, at a wedding or at Easter. It would probably feel the same attending an orgy. I found that after I had sat at the corrida within yards of the woman who ran the launderette, and had seen her cheeks flush a dull Rioja at the moment when the sword drove in, and the moist imprint left on her seat as she rose to fan herself in between bulls, it was difficult ever to think of her in the same way again, to greet her in quite the same cheery manner by the soap dispenser.

It wasn't done to squeal or hide your eyes. Squeamishness was a pale, milky thing. The women were particularly bloodthirsty. They dressed up to the nines and tucked lace handkerchiefs up their sleeves. You didn't wear trousers. You carried a hat. If you found a torero particularly pleasing, for whatever reason, though it was meant to be for his grace and prowess, you cast your handkerchief into the ring and he would turn his back on the bull, showing him his tightly hosed buttocks in an act of bravado bordering on madness, since it invited not only danger but also indignity.

Life in a village has these strange moments of taut inhalation, where the collective breast constricts. Any piece of theatre is more genuinely collective in the round than in a classic row-behind-row auditorium. In the amphitheatre nothing is invisible, even from the cheapest seats. At the outer lip you can still hear the slightest scuff of the matador's ballet-shod toe in the sand, the noise of a nervous *banderillero* clearing his throat behind his hand. The only difference is that if you are in the front row you are much more likely to get charged by the bull. It is the nervous bulls who leap over the rail and into the crowd. They aren't charging, but fleeing, so the best thing is to open up a route for them, and not stand in their way.

The solemnity crushes and uplifts you. The matador is often a fiddling little dandy in his silk suit of pink and blue, but he is also a Promethean, and prepared to die in the course of a common Saturday afternoon. People say that the odds are not equal. The picadors have the look of tobacco-chewing roués who have spent nine years in gaol for rape and are off for a first night back on the town. They entice the bulls up to the flanks of the horse and then stab them, creating huge loss of blood. The justification given is that, were it not for this particular manoeuvre, the matador would have no way of assessing the charge of the bull. There are bulls who simply do not want to fight, who will put their horns down on the ground and scratch at the sand with their hind legs. Then all the boos and whistles are for the man who has raised the bulls; he is in disgrace with the crowd and the matador alike. It is not the bull who is booed. Nobody wants to see a bull put in the ring who has no fight in him.

There are religious overtones only in so far as there is an awareness of death. Death in the afternoon, as Hemingway noticed, will always have a ring about it that is more sinister and disturbing than death at twilight or death in the small hours. As the crowd shouts '*Olé!*' the sense of collaboration between matador and spectator increases. Few people actually understand the movements the matador makes, but they know when he is placing himself in danger and when he isn't.

A bull is an unpredictable animal, and the torero's skill lies in predicting him. Most bulls don't charge exactly when you expect them to. Even a bull who appears to have no fight in him at all will make one crazed charge at some time during the twenty minutes – the entire length of a bull's training period. Before this he has had no contact with the mind of man. People say this is further evidence of the unfairness of the proceedings, but it doesn't take a very sophisticated understanding of the process of evolution to work out that fairness simply doesn't come into it. A man is not as strong as a bull. A bull is not as clever as a man. It is true that the torero has spent his life training for this, ever since, as a child, he first flailed his shirt in the plaza between school and supper shouting '*Toro! Toro! Toro!*' at his obliging younger sister as she scrambled in the dust, practising the various movements that can fool a bull, entice him and destabilize him, in short, lead him where he does not want to go. The bull has not been given this opportunity. Nobody told him that one day he would be required to flout death, to outfox this stripling dandy, whose smell he has probably never encountered before, whose weapons he has never seen, whose speed and agility he has had no chance to measure, whose rules and procedures he must work out even in the moment of combat. But then a man doesn't have horns.

There is no point talking about fairness. It is true that the torero saddles the bull with all sorts of handicaps. He places him in an alien environment, confuses him with music and fanfares and the smell of his fellow creatures' blood, dazzles him with colours and meaningless gestures, and gets other people to make lacerations in his flesh, through which his blood gushes and squirts, alarming, angering and weakening him. At the same time it is the torero's job to display the bull's magnificence to the crowd, to bring out the best and bravest and most powerful in him, and a good torero will do a good job of making his adversary's strong points apparent. In the end the man will say he is a man, and that he has every right to employ whatever skills are particular to his species to subdue and ultimately annihilate the bull. After all, he could just spray the beast with bullets or tranquillizers, if he chose. The absence of technology is important. The man will rely on nothing but his prowess, his own acquired skills. The combat is as equal as it can be while still remaining a combat. The man has his sword and his brain, the bull his horns and his might. Sometimes a bull will display more intelligence than the man, and sometimes the man may not be very good at using his sword.

The most important feature of the bullfight is that it is conducted in public, in the middle of a town, before a thoroughly mixed public. There is nothing clandestine or elitist about it, and the matador is quite likely to die in the demonstration of his skill. If the bull gets hold of him between the ribs and punctures his lungs no-one will step out with a gun and shoot the animal, they will only try to lure him away with coloured scarves.

Everyone is exhausted by the time the sixth bull has been towed from the ring, and the matadors are awarded their accolades: an ear, two ears, an ear and a tail. The carcasses are driven down to the butchers, where there will be queues the following morning, for the corrida bulls are a delicacy, and it is the done thing to invite your neighbours to taste your corrida stew. They say that it has a different taste to abattoir beef, because of the hormones the bulls secrete during the combat – a taste of fear and the hormone that makes the blood boil. The crowd disperses, fluttering with the sense of having witnessed something the rest of the world has ignored. Later there is a meeting at the Salle de Spectacle, where the aficionados analyse the corrida step by step. Then everyone, without exception, goes out and gets drunk.

Visitors

Luc was peeling sycamore twigs to make the *égouttoir*. The windows were wide open onto the late evening, so the mountain was our guest. We were discussing the future.

I said, 'Sometimes this feels like an odd place for me to be.'

Luc looked surprised. It was the most normal place on earth. It was home. 'Maybe this is just *your* place.'

'Why should it be my place?'

'Because *I'm* here.'

'When I was little my father used to take a blank piece of paper and write on the bottom, 'A cow eating grass'. I'd say, 'Where's the grass?' And he'd say, 'The cow's eaten it.' And then I'd say, 'Where's the cow?' And he'd say, 'It's eaten all the grass, so it's gone away.'

'Yes,' Luc said, 'but what would have happened if you'd said, "Where's the cow?" first?'

'It didn't work if you did that.'

I didn't go to Scotland, but flew back to London again in July. One lunchtime I met up with a friend. She had a boyfriend who every time she moved cities to be with him got posted again. Each time she neatly gave in her notice, applied for a new job, and moved to wherever he'd disappeared to this time. Now she was off to

Edinburgh in a hired van. She invited me to lunch at Mezzo – she had saved up vouchers cut out of a Sunday paper and we had a weekday lunch for five pounds each. Chloë was energetic, choosing her sesame roll with care, sending back the water – it was the wrong kind – asking for her vegetables to be served on a separate plate. I thought, I used to be like that. Then I thought, If I don't get out now I'll never get out. I'd rung a number I'd found in an ad in a magazine the day before. The advert said, 'Lovely sunny room in north London.' The woman had said, 'Come over tomorrow at three.' That morning I'd thought, Don't be stupid, you live in France now, with Luc. He's bad tempered, but also good tempered. You've been with him too long, burned too many bridges because of him, tailored yourself to him, cared what he thought, ached for him, bought a house to be near him, moved countries. And now you're going to see a room near Hampstead Heath? But because Chloë was so positive about her rolls and her boyfriend, I walked to the tube at Goodge Street in the summer rain and took the Northern Line.

I rang the bell of a huge house near the hill. A child with solemn eyes pulled open the door. A woman with a beautiful face and grey, lit-up eyes quite unlike her daughter's came forwards, drying her hands on a towel. I told her I'd ring her from France by the end of the month.

All that summer, while my house was rented out to visitors, the farm was full of friends, who came for three or four days, ate with us, drank, re-acquainted themselves with the feelings they'd had the last time they were here, and left.

Marcel came and spent the night with his girlfriend, a beautiful Mexican woman in her sixties, who ran the computer programming section of an airline. She was upset because one of her employees had hanged himself and left a note blaming her for overworking him. Luc said it could have been worse: he could have flown an airplane into a mountain. The programmer had shown admirable restraint. We were all due to meet up at a concert at the monastery on the Sunday night, but my lodgers had a problem with the gas in the house, so I didn't make it. Afterwards Marcel said, 'Luc was looking for you.' It seemed like a sentence I'd never heard before and would never hear again. Luc said, 'You didn't come,' and Marcel said, 'It often happens, that we expect her, and she doesn't arrive.' I thought, Why didn't somebody mention that before?

Friends of mine came to stay in the summer house next door. The children climbed trees. The girls made up dances on the terrace, skipping left and right, then running off after lizards. They hung their washing from the windows and stayed out late at night on the terrace, drinking wine, with the children asleep on their knees. They were so happy they felt like they would stay for ever, and they never quite unpacked. Luc's father came and looked on, never entering the house, just watching from the car, with the poodle yapping at flies in the passenger seat.

Luc was sometimes a good host. In a restaurant one Sunday evening, at the end of a hot day, Aurilly, the elderly dealer from Marseilles, was telling us a story about eating rats during the war. Both Luc and I were tired and only half listening, because we'd heard it before and it was one of those stories you are quite pleased to hear come round again, but feel no obligation to listen to in detail. But we sat up sharp when we realized Aurilly had trailed off in mid-sentence. His head sagged and the hand holding his cigarette fell to the table. Luc plucked the cigarette out of his fingers, and shook him gently, saying his name.

I thought, Oh no, he's dead, but after about half a minute he opened his eyes, which were the same ashy grey as his skin and eyebrows.

He said, 'Where am I?'

Luc said, 'You're in the restaurant in the Rue St Florian. It's Sunday evening. Look, here's your cigarette.'

He said, 'Have I been gone long?'

When you are that old, the loss of time must be very frightening, because it is the thing you most fear about death, that time will no longer be the same.

'No,' Luc said, holding up his cigarette. It had burned about a third of the way down. 'Look, you were only gone from there . . . to there.'

Aurilly recovered, though he still had lapses of consciousness from time to time. My stomach pains got worse. In the pizzeria one lunchtime, Henri said, 'Why aren't you eating? Have you got palpitations? Low blood sugar? Are you depressed? Tired? *Neurasthénique? Cholérique?* Why don't you go to the clinic?' The French are always interested in illness. In England illness is seen as less-than-wellness, a falling short of the normal state of things. The French think of illness without intrinsic value attached, so it can be made quite positive, interesting, just as an account of a disaster can be made into an exciting piece of writing. A Portuguese poet who was staying with Luc grabbed my arm and shouted, 'I am taking you there now myself!' At the next table sat Laurent, head of radiology at the clinic. He peered through shaggy eyebrows, waved his spoon and said, 'Come at the end of the afternoon and we'll check you out.'

I went and lay down on the machines, removing, in response to Laurent's instructions, all sorts of bits of clothing that could hardly have impeded the photographic process, and staring up at the ceiling thinking, Maybe these are my last hours of not knowing I'm ill. Enjoy it. It was difficult to enjoy it, though, as Laurent was pointing the machines at parts of me which even my rudimentary knowledge of physiology and pathology told me had no connection with the pain. The consultant came in and looked at the pictures and said, 'Very nice. No problem,' and left for the beach for the weekend. Laurent came and placed his hand on my breast and said, 'Does it hurt there?' Paralysed, I felt nothing at all, and then a nurse came in and Laurent leapt back and started writing out notes.

I went and finished my shopping, to add to what Luc kept in his store cupboard, the sum of which was always just short of a meal. He stockpiled sunflower oil, white sugar cubes, eggs, pasta, rice and matches. Anything after that was detail. Whenever you went to the supermarket it took ten minutes to spend around 400 francs. It always seemed to cost 400 francs, whatever you put in the trolley, which at least made housekeeping easy.

When I got to the café in the early evening, sitting at the round table on the terrace were Luc and his friends, Morgan, my current lodger, an American academic with a strangely inverted face and a different little black dress for every day of the week, and Laurent and two of his technicians from the lab. The only place free was next to Laurent. I sat down and he put his arm round me, and said, 'We looked after you, didn't we, *coquine*,' and Luc said, 'Is she OK then?' Laurent squeezed my shoulder and said, 'She's fine. Maybe come back in a couple of months for another look.'

Morgan came up to the farm with me and we prepared the food on the terrace. The Portuguese poet tried to peel the green beans. He said that was what they did in his country, but he was clearly confusing them with something else. I leaned over to pour salt in the water and he stopped my arm and said, 'I have been weeping. It is enough,' and Morgan said, 'Hey, Mr Organic, have some more red wine and pee in the salad dressing, could you?'

An exhibition of Picasso's drawings had just opened in the village, so there were lots of painters around, and journalists and poets, just hanging out for a while. I thought that evening, as we sat on the terrace and ate, that I'd never seen such a collection of beautiful men in my life; you'd have thought it was some kind of convention. It seemed to me that day that men were more beautiful than women, when they were beautiful at all. The Portuguese poet looked like a Roman who has had extremely successful cosmetic surgery, so the nose was that bit more chiselled, the cheekbones that bit sharper, his teeth just plain white and his skin a perfect mixture of soft and stubbled. Real Clinique advert standard. My favourite, a doctor in his late fifties, looked like Paul Tortelier crossed with Samuel Beckett. He had spent a lot of time abroad working for Médecins Sans Frontières, which put him right at the top of my list of Mills & Boon heroes.

Luc grilled the tuna steaks on the fire, with his back to everyone and the dog at his feet. Morgan's black dress rode up high round her thighs, and she sat on the wall and watched the horses grazing, unconsciously imitating their expressions. Charles, a painter from Nice, was watching Morgan, unconsciously imitating hers. He had been one of those outside the café on the day of Luc's exhibition, when I'd passed by with my Walkman. Since then I'd put him in a book I'd written in Luc's house, because he had pale-blue eyes and a shambolic face, though now the flesh was starting to fall, so it looked like a garment hastily slung onto a hanger.

Charles's wife was a teacher, extremely dynamic, a classic French mother of almost-grown children, hyper-manicured, who shopped in heels. Charles himself was a copywriter, but had recently been discovered by Luc's gallery and was doing well. Soon, he hoped, he would be able to give up advertising and paint full time in the studio at the bottom of the garden in their newly built house in the Vaucluse.

'It would be a catastrophe for him,' Luc said.

It was true. Charles needed his cage, or he'd stop rattling and produce nothing. Occasionally he'd turn up with a lover, a manicurist twenty years younger than him. She had a poodle. Charles would phone Luc and say, 'I have to get away from these women, I'm going mad. Can I come?' and Luc would say, 'Of course. Come this weekend. We'll have a men's weekend.' In between his phone call and the weekend, Charles would make it up with the manicurist and they would arrive together and lock themselves in a bedroom with a view of the mountain for three days. Luc would meet Charles on the way to the bathroom, with the manicurist's robe clutched around him, frothing prettily at the collar. When Luc was single, and waiting for a woman to parachute into his life, he found these men's weekends particularly trying, and usually ended up taking his horse and leaving a note on the fridge door for the manicurist, telling her where to find the eggs and rice. When he came back on the Sunday night they'd have gone, leaving a note saying they'd gone to eat fish at the port and would see him soon. But this time Charles had come alone.

Luc moved around, doing the things that had to be done every night on the farm. Next door the lights were still on, though Georges, Luc's brother, usually went to bed before nine. He had signed up with a dating agency a year after Brigitte left, and after a few distant misses had been introduced to Emilie, who was in her early forties, pretty, with rosy cheeks and a gentle, scolding voice, and a very small child called Léo. Luc said if Georges ever got the private investigator onto her we could call it Emilie and the Detectives. Emilie was a trained seamstress, and had put her sewing machine where Brigitte's piano had been. She had also brought a seamstress's dummy, which she stood in the window, draped in sleeveless coats and half-finished jackets, a ghostly rural equivalent of Gigi's shop window. Georges adored Léo, and carried him everywhere. Luc would watch them crossing the field together and wonder if he could do that, too. Somehow Georges had stepped out ahead of him and stolen his plan. The one thing he might really have wanted, his brother had done first, and now he didn't want it as much as he had before.

The sun had gone behind the mountain, but it was still light, as though the horizon kept slipping an inch and it would never quite grow dark. When the horses drank from the manger in the stable, the water chugged in the pipes, and it sounded the way it does when children noisily suck up the last of their juice through a straw. Luc was telling a story. That morning he had been fixing a crown on a patient's tooth. The patient had kept on asking for more anaesthetic. Luc had a reputation for pain-free treatment. Some people, the old mayor included, had such faith in him, they insisted on being treated without anaesthetic, even for extractions. My father had always insisted that his dentist do his fillings without anaesthetic, because he said it was worth it in order to be able to taste his lunch afterwards. It would have been simpler to have his dental appointments after lunch, but I think he enjoyed it that way. That morning's patient had been anaesthetized to the very limit one mouth could take

233

when he started to cough. 'Cigarettes,' he said, with rubberized consonants, and opened his mouth once again. The crown had gone. 'Quick,' Luc said. 'Open wide.' He stuck his fingers in, probed around and found nothing. He tipped the patient's head forward. Still nothing. Nothing rattled, or fell. *Merde*, he thought, and stuck his fingers down the patient's throat. Nothing. He asked if he'd felt anything. Nothing at all, the patient assured him. He was fine. Luc rang Laurent at the clinic. 'I'm sending you someone,' he said. 'A patient's swallowed a crown.' An X-ray confirmed that the patient, a forester, had a crown in his stomach. Eat lots of bread, they told him, and watch out for unusually difficult stools. That morning the patient had rung, triumphant as a child who's found a coin in a Christmas pudding. Would Luc like to have it back?

'Good bloke, Laurent,' Luc said, looking at me. '*N'est-ce pas?*'

The next morning Morgan and Charles were up first, claiming not to have gone to bed. Morgan had panda eyes, wild with mascara. Luc shut himself up in his atelier. He was designing the dish drainer, he said. I took him a beer at midday. The drainer was huge, more like something Robert the Bruce and his chieftains might have stacked their shields in. All that day and all the next, a Sunday, Morgan and Charles sat on a bench under a lime tree in the garden, Charles sketching, Morgan looking riveted, as though with his next breath he might be about to divulge the secret of where the treasure was hidden, which you didn't have to know Charles very well to realize was unlikely. Luc got frustrated with his carpentry and tossed it into the stable for the horses to scratch themselves on, and spent the rest of the day stalking around the farm in his ripped jeans and riding boots, looking for a lost chisel in the grass. His slender chest was black brown from the sun, his eyes like dark acacia honey. 'What's up?' I asked. He said he was sick of people who came to spend time on the farm *par exotisme*. 'They lie around, they make love, they admire the view through the window, then they go again. They use it as a back-drop. They bring their own stupid concerns with them and pump away at them under my roof.' He hated adolescent flirtation in adults, coy looks and innuendo under the lime tree. At least Charles had made the manicurist scream with pleasure.

Eventually, on the Sunday evening, Luc invited some friends over, so Morgan had to go back to the village. They said goodbye at the gate, and Charles walked slowly back down the drive, looking sad and important. Luc put on Jimi Hendrix very loud and began drilling a hole in the wall to attach a new coat peg for the hat he'd bought in Figueras market.

Our friends arrived for dinner, people from Paris, the parents of Chloë of the sesame rolls. They had a farm on the other side of the valley, where they spent several weeks a year. They arrived at seven, because they never liked to stay late. They were urbane, pro-fessional people in their late fifties, with high-up jobs in the art world, the only 'intellectuals' Luc tolerated. He adored them, but still thought their life was berserk – all that culture, all that walking the streets of Paris, *les pauvres*.

The light always seemed different in that room on summer Sunday evenings, more golden. We ate chicken and rice and salad at the oval table. The potager was at its height, with five different types of lettuce. We probably ate too much salad that summer – maybe that was the problem with my digestion. Charles was thrilled to meet Luc's Parisian friends, and was shy and charming. At one point Eugène asked him how the painting was going, and Charles replied that he had just had a show in the Rue de Seine.

'I know,' Eugène said, 'I saw it.' Charles had already complained to Luc earlier that these smart Parisian people with influence never went to any contemporary shows; they never really knew what was going on.

'Of course,' he said. 'Of course, I'm sure you did.'

'You were on the left, in the second room,' Eugène said, which was true, and shut Charles up until, when Stéphanie asked Luc how his surgery was going, he decided to make up for his fault by telling the story of the swallowed crown.

It was a difficult story to tell badly. It wasn't till I started clearing the plates that I noticed Luc hadn't spoken for half an hour. When Eugène and Stéphanie left, we saw them off and walked back to the house together. Luc went to close the gates and Charles and I began washing up. It was still quite early. Luc came in and poured himself a drink.

He saluted Charles ironically. '*Bravo*,' he said. '*Merci, cher ami.*'

Charles smiled anxiously. 'What? What for?'

There was a silence, then Luc burst open like a spraying firework, everything shooting outwards in fury, with crackers popping round his feet. Charles had let him down in front of his friends. Here Luc was, trying to earn a decent living, entertaining his friends, his girlfriend cooking for everyone, providing them with a location for their smutty teen affairs. They, and most particularly Charles – and he hated artists – were posers and fakes, and he never wanted to see Charles again. He could just get lost, get out of his sight. 'And you,' he said to me. 'You didn't stop him. You're supposed to defend me. I don't know whose side you're on. Why didn't you interrupt him? You can just

236

get back to your own world, too. I'm not a tourist attraction. Won't be turned into one.'

He went to bed.

Charles debated whether he should go and spend the night in my house with Morgan, and decided against it. Men, once they pass thirty, are surprisingly prudent in their arrangements. He left in the morning and Luc predicted that the manicurist would be getting a nice surprise around midday. We were sitting reading that evening when Luc began to giggle. It started somewhere at the top of his head and worked its way down his body. I sat there thinking, I am sitting here opposing his laughter. Nothing's funny. What's going on?

He said, 'Charles's face! Marcel will piss himself when I tell him.'

'No, he won't,' I said. 'He'll think, There's Luc again, getting away with it because he won't condemn himself.' It was like listening to the gospel story of the adulterous woman, if you made the exchange between her and Christ into a comic monologue. Jesus says, 'Where are all thine accusers?' and she says, 'Gone Lord,' and he says, 'Then neither do I accuse you.' Luc would look around and say, 'Who accuses me?' and they'd all have gone running because they loved him and wouldn't fight with him, and so he'd shrug and say, 'They obviously thought I was all right all along.'

I'd try to get him to see how much harm he did: 'You *can't* believe it's OK to say the things you do.' One night he'd rung up a woman in her eighties, the one who called his waiting room a bathroom, and told her down the phone she was a fat-arsed, gossiping tart. Only one out of the three terms was strictly untrue. Afterwards he'd said, 'She didn't really mind. Look, she still comes running.' And indeed she had at once come running, with pots of jam and truffles to soothe his nerves, to make up to him because his *maman* had died. Because no-one ever berated him to his face, he believed he had done nothing wrong. He would never blame himself, and the myth of his blamelessness grew like scales over everyone's eyes.

I said to Luc, 'I'm leaving. I've found a room in London. I'm going to go and live there for a while.'

'What's so special about it then? Why this room, now?'

'There's a piano. I don't think I can spend another winter here.'

'*C'est bien*,' he said. 'I always knew you'd leave.'

'That's why I'm leaving,' I said. 'Because you keep saying I will. Now it's come true.'

'Then I was right,' he said.

I wrapped up my bike in brown paper and took it to the train station. I had a huge rucksack, too. I thought, I'm too old to be at a train station with a rucksack and a bicycle, crying, again. I thought I could still turn back, and go and sleep on the farm and wake up to the sound of the horses drinking from the trough below the terrace. The station master said, 'I don't know who you spoke to on the phone, but you certainly can't bring that bike on here.'

Luc came awake for the first time that day. He put his arms round me and said, 'Don't cry, *coquine*, you can always come back,' and put my bike on the train anyway, where the staff treated it like a pet and patted it each time they went up and down the corridor.

London

What happened then? Princess Diana was killed in a country that seemed to have nothing to do with the country I'd been living in, as though it had happened in an underworld that bore no relation to the everyday world above. That was the day I arrived back in London, in the big house with the children. They were the kind of children I'd dreamed about meeting when I was small. They lived in a rambling house, wore jeans and hand-knitted blue jumpers, kept insects in matchboxes and spent summers playing in and out of rock pools and waves on a Cornish beach. Everyone played music. I sat on my bed with my rucksack on the floor. I wondered if it was possible to change like this, just to wrench yourself out of one place and, by physically going to another, consider yourself to have moved. It was the most beautiful day of the summer, just at the end. It reminded me of early autumn Sunday evenings, when my father used to take me and my brother back to university with our trunks. They were flying Diana's coffin back to London. They were playing English music and people were walking stiffly and sadly on the television. I began unpacking my rucksack, and the little boy came in and said there was a postcard for me from America, and would I mind if he steamed off the stamp.

It was a time when nothing had quite ended, because nothing new had begun. At night, in London, I lay awake wondering if I should be there. I was living in a half-world, where everything was more unfamiliar to me than anything in France had ever been. London had become so fancy. It had so many chic Italian and French restaurants, patisseries and delis, it almost felt like America. I wrote to Luc from my desk in the Round Reading Room, letters in green ink which I never posted. I read a book called *Why Women Write More Love Letters Than They Post*.

He never wrote. Once I'd said to him, 'You never write to me. I don't even know your handwriting.'

He said, 'Which hand do I write with?'

'Left'.

'No,' he said. 'Right. What hand do I draw with?'

'Right.'

'No, left.'

'What colour are my eyes?' I asked.

'Green. And I know that', he said, 'because Gigi said to me the other day, "She had beautiful blue eyes, your English girl," and I realized there was something wrong with the sentence.'

It's true. If you have green eyes, only the people who really like you notice they're green and not blue.

'You've still never written me a letter.'

I went out to the garden to pick salad leaves, and when I came back in there was a Kit-Kat wrapper with its white inside facing up, trapped under a stone on the kitchen table. He'd written, '*Coucou, coquine*. Luc.' I've kept it, and I tell myself it's a love letter, but I expect in five years' time I'll change my mind and throw it away.

Irene Bishop wrote from North Carolina to finalize her plans. She would be in Paris for a week, then she would travel down by train to the house. Luc and I spoke twice a week on the phone. We still half believed this was just an interlude, like the ones we'd known before. He said, 'You have to get this book you've written out of the way. You have to stop *wanting* things so much.' I said to him on the phone, 'The woman who wrote is coming from America. She's seventy-seven. She's staying for three weeks. Can you meet her at the train station? She'll need someone to carry her luggage. It's difficult, travelling when you're old.'

'She should stay at home then,' he said.

So the night before the Saturday she was due, only two months after I'd left, I flew to Gerona; Luc picked me up and we drove back to the village. He looked me up and down and said, 'Your clothes are different.'

I said, 'Well, I've been temping all week to get the plane fare.'

'What's temping?'

We were sitting in the crêperie, late at night. Luc had stopped drinking, he said, so it was a bit gloomy, sitting there with our water, trying to find things to talk about. 'How's your father?'

'Very well.'

'The horses?'

'Fine.'

'I'm writing an article about love letters for a magazine.'

'Ha.'

Laurent came in to buy cigarettes. '*Ça va?*'

It was hot the next day when I took Luc's car and drove from the farm to Perpignan railway station. The floor of the Land-Rover was littered with my old tapes. Luc had kept everything of mine as it had been. It felt weird, like someone who doesn't accept a person has died, and keeps their room just as it has always been and won't give their clothes away. The car smelled of hay that's been dried behind glass over a hot summer. It smelled of old dog, too, and of the leather of the horses' saddles, and there were odd bits of free samples from pharmaceutical companies, and gallery invitations on the dashboard, and the odd single riding glove, and my leather riding jacket hanging over the bar in the back. I switched on the tape recorder. It was halfway through Blur singing about people going home through the suburbs after a night out in London. Luc had been listening to it without understanding the words. Or maybe he did. It turned out he spoke really good English, so other people told me, though he never spoke it to me. Once he said in English to a friend of mine from London who he'd met in the market, 'I am told that you are a metalwork restorer in the area of fine art. But do you only restore existing pieces or do you create sculpture of your own?' which was an unusual first sentence, I thought.

The motorway slides alongside the sea. I was held up at the *péage*, and the train, which must have dropped Irene Bishop at the station, passed me between the road and the sea. The vine fields were lime gold, the leaves dark red-wine stained here and there, though in fact that was just the colour they turned in autumn and nothing to do with the colour of the wine. The sky was an uncomplicated blue. There was no snow yet on the mountain. At the station Irene was standing a head above the crowd in narrow tartan trousers. She had steel-grey short hair. She was holding a piece of paper with my name on. It seemed to correspond with the little I knew of her, that the piece of paper should bear my name and not hers.

I drove her back to the village. I tried to drive slowly, because the train would have been so fast. She told me she had stayed in a hotel in Paris where she'd last stayed in the Fifties, with her husband. They had taken a trip

242

down this way one summer in a car whose engine had overheated. She talked about 'writing programmes' and the fall. I took her to the house, then went and did some shopping for her, and some for me, too, and we met up at the Café Central for a sandwich. She said she needed to rest for two days. I said I had to go back to London on Thursday. 'Then come and see me,' she said, 'on Wednesday at midday.'

Luc said, 'She looks deranged.' I didn't think she looked at all deranged. She looked beautiful and clever, and she was as tall as a stork. 'I don't think you understand,' I said.

'You're right,' he replied. 'I don't. Are you going to come back?'

'I don't know. Maybe. I don't like London much. I love it here.'

'When your book's over, come back. We'll have a family.'

I'd heard it all before, but I let it drift. Bits of his talk, his dreams, settled on me like dust I didn't want to wash away. We rode down the familiar paths in the forest. I had become again a person who rode on escalators and watched the adverts skim by. My horse, Hector, was quiet, stepping carefully through the first fallen leaves, though the forest was still dark green within, only the edges singed with autumn. Early autumn leaves are the ones the sun has sizzled, and they crack more sharply underfoot. I could have ridden through the forest with my eyes shut and known after a few seconds what season it was, just from the noise the horse's hooves made on the ground. In winter they made a 'clock-clock' sound, as though the earth were hollow inside. Maybe Luc had had a word with Hector and said, 'Don't play up. Do this for me.' The dog was also subdued. Not particularly pleased to see me, either. In the village everyone said, *'Tiens*, you're back.' They never said, 'How's London?' they just said, 'Isn't it marvellous! How you must have missed it!'

On my last day I went round to the house at noon. Irene was out on the terrace. She was reading a book. She waved it at me. 'My doctor says I shouldn't sit in the sun, but if I can't sit in the sun, what's left? Have you read this? Take it. Write to me. Tell me what you think.'

I've always felt happy around old people, and not just because they make me feel young. The children from the garden next door came home from school at lunchtime. The little girl began her piano practice. The two boys ran out with a ball into the garden. They had a new game, where one of them sat in the crook of the peach tree and threw the ball at the other one's head. The woman next door with no teeth was baking fish with herbs. Irene said, 'It's too good to move,' so I went and bought two huge plates of Greek salad from Angélique's bar. Luc was there with Serge Collier. The social services had taken Serge's two small foster twins away that morning and returned them to their natural mother. 'I always knew I'd have to let them go,' he said. 'But it's so harsh and sudden. We have no visiting rights.'

'*Quelle époque*,' Luc said. 'Can I get you a coffee, *coquine*?'

I said I was visiting the woman in the house.

'Again?'

'This is the first time,' I said. 'The other time I was only picking her up. After all, I came all this way to see her.'

'*Ah bon.* I thought you came to see me.'

Gigi came up and slid onto a stool next to Luc. 'Hello, stranger,' she said, looking at me, 'you've lost some weight.'

'You always say that,' Luc said, for which I was

grateful. 'Can't you think of anything else to say?' It was the first time I'd seen him irritable with Gigi.

'Two salads,' Angélique said.

Two salads nearer the Dominican Republic. She leaned back against the espresso machine. 'How's London?'

Gigi said, 'You look *très chic*. No more ripped jeans, then? Isn't that Agnès B.?'

'Where?' said Luc, looking up and down the street. He was always interested in new women arriving in town.

'On her back.'

'*Where?*'

I went back to the house. Irene had moved into the shade. I found plates and cutlery and little glasses. We had a glass of wine each. She said, 'My doctor also says no wine, but what's life if there's no wine?'

She spoke about her son, who might have been a painter but had stopped painting. 'He has a nice wife. He went into teaching when he married, but they've never had children. Now they're building a house. When it's finished, he says, he'll start to paint again, but they won't because the house he's building's not that sort of house. Time goes by. He says he's writing a book.'

A couple of hours later I stood at the top of the stairs and noticed that the smell of the sixteen cats had gone. She said, 'I won't see you again, but I will write. Write to me. Tell me what you decide to do.' She handed me some postcards. 'Post these for me.'

I ran down the stairs and out into the street. I felt sad but elated. She opened the kitchen window and called down to me from the first floor. I squinted up at her, dizzy out in the light. 'Read the top one,' she said. It was addressed to her son. It said, 'She is kind and clever. She does not seem to know how happy she

245

could be.' When I looked back up at the window she'd gone, as though I'd imagined her in the first place. I expect she had gone to lie down in my white room with the blue shutters. What did an old woman look like lying between the sheets with the shutters drawn in the early afternoon? I posted the cards and drove to the beach, where I met a friend and swam in the sea.

I left and he said, 'Come back when you've finished. Nothing's decided yet. I'm not going anywhere.'

One afternoon I was in the library and I suddenly thought, I have to tell him now, though I didn't usually ring him in the afternoon. I went out to the shop and bought an eraser with the British Library stamp on it to get some small change, and I called him from the phones at the exit to the old Reading Room in the British Museum, where there are always students ringing for flats or trying to track down someone in Earls Court who they met years before on a bus in Jerusalem.

'Luc?'

'Yes.'

'Luc . . .'

He said, 'I can't talk. The dog's just died.'

He never wept when his mother died, but he wept for a week over his dog. He said, 'Are you coming back now?'

I closed my eyes and said, 'I can't.'

'You tell me this *now*, when the dog's died?'

'Well, yes,' I said.

I wanted to say that worse things had happened to people, that the first time he'd dumped me it had been three weeks before my divorce came through. When you realize someone needs you to assuage their un-happiness, an unhappiness you didn't create, and you would gladly do it, but you know they shouldn't build a new life on the hope of you, you have to go. I wanted to say that his dog dying was beside the point. He had no pity for other people, but suddenly his dog had died and he thought there should be some kind of state funeral.

'Why are you telling me now?'

'I couldn't *not* tell you and have you think it would be all right, the dog dying, because I'd come back.'

'You never liked her,' he said. 'She told me.'

A week later he rang me and said, 'People are very interested in the village. You're quite a celebrity here. I've told them you've left, of course. Everyone said, "She looked like such a sweet girl." Gigi wasn't surprised, though. She said she'd known you all along. She says you're like her, that it's something she could have done when she was your age. She never trusted you. She always said you'd leave once I told you I needed you here.'

'I thought it was you who said that. You said it every day. That's why I left. You know that.'

'Gigi told me you would. She knows women. She can read you like a book.'

'She needs glasses,' I said.

'She wears them for reading now,' he said. 'In bed.'

I said, 'Irene died.' I'd got back from a weekend in Cornwall with the children and the rock pools and I'd found an e-mail from her son.

'Who?'

'The woman who came to my house.'

'She was old.'

'Not old enough, though.'

'None of us is ever that,' he said.

I returned to the village once more the following March. Luc and I met in the street one night. He looked alone, as though something was missing. I realized it was the dog. It was a dark night, no moon, only the

247

ghastly orange light of the street lamps. The mountain was hidden by cloud, the cafés were closed, but even if they'd been open we wouldn't have gone and sat at the bar and drunk a beer. It was one of the rights I'd forfeited by leaving, one of many. We walked, talked stiffly. We no longer knew how long each other's sentences were going to last. We were both terribly unhappy. We knew, too, that in a few minutes we'd part. Outside my house, he stopped. 'I'm going to sell it,' I said. I couldn't keep it and not be with him. I'd bought it so I'd never have to leave the village, but I'd left anyway, so as not to be with him.

'Why do that?' he asked. 'It's a pretty house. You like it. Don't sell it because of me.'

I said, 'It's too big.'

I meant too big for me. I felt so small and far away, it seemed vast and unmanageable. It would change and decay in the weather, while I sat in the library in London, under the sheltering dome.

Luc squinted at me. 'Too small, you mean.'

'What?'

'Too small. You want a family. Children and cats and books and visitors. Now you say the house is too big. Get it straight in your head, *coquine*.' He pushed himself off from against the wall, where he'd been leaning back with the flat of one foot against the stone, and walked off down the street. I rang Monsieur Barthieu the next morning, and within two weeks the house was sold to some Swedes who were as flat and flavourless as a smorgasbord. I left them a sack of white lime paint for the walls.

6. Leaving

There's so much less to say about leaving than arriving. Everything's familiar by now. Rubbish goes in the big plastic bins in the car park. Marianne comes and cleans on Saturday at midday. Make sure the shutters are hooked back and the windows bolted fast. Leave the towels and the sheets in the bedrooms, where they are. Lock the inside door at the top of stairs, and leave the keys in the hole in the wall by the postbox to the right of the door.

I leave by car, on a day that is neither autumn nor winter. The village is already behind me, in the nape of the hills that ripple down to its outer walls, a pile of warm yellow and pink stone. It sits like a newborn child, wrapped in the folds of these protecting slopes, a pleat in the landscape, ageing, changing, imperceptibly to human eyes. But it is never not here. It is we who leave, forget, return, change, we the visitors. The Pont du Diable is grey in the afternoon light. On the disused railway bridge is a flat silhouette of a bull, made of tin. The green municipal bins are being emptied, and a lorry is spraying fluorescent dotted markings on the road. When I stop at the roundabout and take one last look, I remind myself this was once, and may always be, my place. I know I'll always misremember something, move a line of trees, forget a twist in the river, cancel a bank of trees or a vital cloud. My mind's eye grows tired. Each time it blinks the landscape shifts a season, passing from mimosa into pale peach pink, to early summer lime and late summer yellows and then orange and red, as though gradually less water were being added to the wine as the year wears on. On my left, as I drive up the slip road, is the mountain Virgil loved, rigid against the banking equinox clouds. I wind down the window, throw my two francs into the wire basket and the barrier lifts. A train passes, going the other way.

PERFUME FROM PROVENCE
Lady Fortescue

'HAS CHARM AND PERIOD FRAGRANCE'
Adam Ruck, *Daily Telegraph*

In the early 1930s, Winifred Fortescue and her husband, Sir John Fortescue, left England and settled in Provence, in a small stone house amid olive groves, on the border of Grasse. Almost at once they were bewitched, by the charming, infuriating, warm-hearted and wily Provençals. The house was delightful but tiny, and at once plans were put in hand to extend it over the mountain terrace. Winifred Fortescue's witty and warm account of life with stonemasons, craftsmen, gardeners, and above all her total involvement with the everyday events of a Provençal village, made *Perfume From Provence* an instant bestseller.

'Lady Fortescue bursts upon the unsuspecting village with unaffected delight, torpedoing the siesta'd somnolence of small-town bureaucrats . . . regally chauffeuring neighbours' wedding guests in the Fortescue Fiat . . . her world centres on house and garden . . . on her bald, fanatical but devoted gardener. The perfume of this Provence may belong to a forgotten age, but thanks to her own undisguised enjoyment, its fragrance charms and lingers still'
City Limits

0 552 99479 0

BLACK SWAN

THE ELUSIVE TRUFFLE
Travels In Search of the Legendary Food of France
Mirabel Osler
Illustrations by Simon Dorrell
Recipes interpreted by Shaun Hill

'IN A CLASS OF ITS OWN'
Mail on Sunday

In years gone by, the traveller in France could rely on coming across a restaurant where the tables were ready-laid with heavy cotton napkins, a carafe of wine and a basket of freshly baked bread, and where the ensuing meal would encompass recipes of remarkable local dishes handed down from generation to generation. But no longer.

In an inspiring quest for this rapidly disappearing traditional cuisine and culture, Mirabel Osler travels the length and breadth of France, focusing on individual chefs and restaurants, exploring producers and suppliers such as the travelling butchers and bakers, It is an enticing and evocative picture of a way of life which is fast being eroded by the modern world, but also an affirmation that, for some, the old traditions will always survive.

'MUCH MORE THAN A COOKERY BOOK, MUCH MORE. IT IS A BEAUTIFULLY ILLUSTRATED TRAVEL BOOK IN IT'S OWN RIGHT WRITTEN BY A HIGHLY INTELLIGENT WOMAN WHO HAS DONE US ALL A FAVOUR'
Mail On Sunday

'ANYONE WHO HAS DRIVEN THROUGH FRANCE WITH THE RED MICHELIN BOOK ON HIS OR HER LAP WILL LOVE *THE ELUSIVE TRUFFLE*'
Richard Ehrlich, *Guardian*

'NOT ONLY A NOSTALGIC TRIP INTO THE PAST BUT A SYMPATHETIC ANALYSIS OF THE FRENCH AT TABLE IN THE AGE OF PROCESSED FOOD. IT MAY MAKE YOU SAD BUT IT WILL ALSO MAKE YOU VERY HUNGRY INDEED'
Derek Cooper

0 552 99852 4

BLACK SWAN

NOTES FROM AN ITALIAN GARDEN
Joan Marble

'THIS DESCRIPTION OF MAKING HEAVEN ON EARTH IS
AN UNLOOKED-FOR DELIGHT'
Independent on Sunday

*'I fell in love with Etruria one chilly evening in January.
They were having a New Year's Eve festival in a little town
near Campagnano, and a group of local boys dressed in
Renaissance costumes were marching in a torchlight
parade down the main street. As I stood there in the cold
watching the flames lurching to the sky, I realised that I felt
very much at home in this ancient place. If ever we should
decide to move to this country, this was the kind of place I
would choose. . .'*

Thirty years ago Joan Marble and her sculptor husband
Robert Cook bought a piece of unpromising land in Lazio,
the area north of Rome that was home to the ancient
Etruscans. They built a house and, more importantly, grew
a wonderful garden. The challenge was both exciting and
daunting, and poor soil, an inhospitable climate and the
blank incomprehension of their neighbours sometimes
made it seem as though they would never realise their
dream. But Joan and Robert's enthusiasm for the land,
their determination and inspiration, and the unexpected
friends who helped them, all served to make the landscape
blossom.

'THIS BOOK IS ALL ADVENTURE. MS MARBLE DOES
SOME DIZZY TRAVELLING. HER ROOF BLOWS OFF. SHE
SURVIVES KILLER WASPS AND POISONOUS PINE MOTHS.
MOST INSPIRING OF ALL SHE REVIVES A WILTING
CLIMBER WITH TWO CUPS OF COLD RICE PUDDING
AND TAKES GERMINATING SEEDS TO DINNER
PARTIES. I WISH I KNEW HER. I LOVE HER BOOK'
Phyllida Law

'A STORY OF A HOME CREATED WITH LOVE AND
PASSION. EVEN NON-GARDENERS WILL FIND IT
ENCHANTING'
Irish News

0 552 99841 9

BLACK SWAN

A SELECTED LIST OF FINE WRITING
AVAILABLE FROM BLACK SWAN

THE PRICES SHOWN BELOW WERE CORRECT AT THE TIME OF GOING TO PRESS. HOWEVER
TRANSWORLD PUBLISHERS RESERVE THE RIGHT TO SHOW NEW RETAIL PRICES ON COVERS WHICH
MAY DIFFER FROM THOSE PREVIOUSLY ADVERTISED IN THE TEXT OR ELSEWHERE.

99927 X	THE STATELY HOMO	ed. Paul Bailey	£8.99
99600 9	NOTES FROM A SMALL ISLAND	Bill Bryson	£6.99
99786 2	NOTES FROM A BIG COUNTRY	Bill Bryson	£7.99
99805 2	MADE IN AMERICA	Bill Bryson	£7.99
99806 0	NEITHER HERE NOR THERE	Bill Bryson	£6.99
99702 1	A WALK IN THE WOODS	Bill Bryson	£6.99
99808 7	THE LOST CONTINENT	Bill Bryson	£6.99
99703 X	DOWN UNDER	Bill Bryson	£7.99
99926 1	DEAR TOM	Tom Courtenay	£7.99
99802 8	DON'T WALK IN THE LONG GRASS	Tenniel Evans	£6.99
99729 3	TRUTH	Felipe Fernández-Armesto	£6.99
99482 0	MILLENNIUM	Felipe Fernández-Armesto	£14.99
99858 3	PERFUME FROM PROVENCE	Lady Fortescue	£6.99
99545 2	ISRAEL: A HISTORY	Martin Gilbert	£14.99
12555 5	IN SEARCH OF SCHRÖDINGER'S CAT	John Gribbin	£7.99
99680 7	THE IMAGINARY GIRLFRIEND	John Irving	£5.99
99868 0	MY MOVIE BUSINESS	John Irving	£6.99
99958 X	ALMOST LIKE A WHALE	Steve Jones	£8.99
14595 5	BETWEEN EXTREMES	Brian Keenan and John McCarthy	£7.99
99841 9	NOTES FROM AN ITALIAN GARDEN	Joan Marble	£7.99
99803 6	THINGS CAN ONLY GET BETTER	John O'Farrell	£6.99
99852 4	THE ELUSIVE TRUFFLE: Travels in Search of the Legendary Food of France	Mirabel Osler	£6.99
99913 X	THE JADU HOUSE: Intimate Histories of Anglo–India	Laura Roychowdhury	£7.99
99750 1	SPEAKING FOR THEMSELVES:	ed. Mary Soames	£15.00
99923 7	THE MYSTERY OF CAPITAL	Hernando De Soto	£7.99
99891 5	IN THE SHADOW OF A SAINT	Ken Wiwa	£6.99

All Transworld titles are available by post from:
Bookpost, PO Box 29, Douglas, Isle of Man, IM99 1BQ
Credit cards accepted. Please telephone 01624 836000,
fax 01624 837033, Internet http://www.bookpost.co.uk
or e-mail: bookshop@enterprise.net for details.
Free postage and packing in the UK. Overseas customers: allow
£1 per book (paperbacks) and £3 per book (hardbacks).